PHOENIX
RISING

TERROR VICTIM TO BURN SURVIVOR

ANTONY SVILICICH

All correspondence to the author:

Email: antony_svilicich@hotmail.com
https://www.linkedin.com/feed/

ISBN: 978-0-6455924-0-5

Proudly produced by

TheBookStudio
www.thebookstudio.com.au

Dedicated to my family – for keeping the faith.

Contents

PREFACE

Bali is an island located on the Indonesian archipelago, approximately 1400 kilometres north of the Australian coastline and a quick three-and-a-half-hour flight from Perth, Western Australia. With its warm tropical climate, great surf breaks and friendly people, Bali is frequented by visitors from all over the world. It is also one of Australia's favourite overseas holiday destinations due to its proximity to the Australian mainland and affordable holiday packages.

On 12 October 2002, the beginning of a series of bombings occurred in Bali. The attacks, in the busy entertainment precinct of Kuta, were carried out by terrorist network Jemaah Islamiyah. These attacks claimed the lives of 202 people, including 88 Australians, and wounded 240 – including me. This book is an account of the attacks in Kuta and the story of my survival, against the odds.

INTRODUCTION

On 12 October 2002, I was in the Sari Club, one of the most popular nightclubs in Kuta, Bali, one of Indonesia's key international tourist destinations. It was a hot, humid night, the music was pumping and everyone was having a good time talking, laughing and dancing.

Sitting behind the sunken bar, I had just struck up conversation with two Australian girls when a deafening explosion rocked the Legian beach strip. I looked south towards Paddy's Bar and saw a black mushroom cloud of smoke rise from the roof.

Someone shouted, 'What the hell was that?'

Only seconds later, the Bintang bottle in my hand shattered as a powerful car bomb ripped apart the Sari Club.

I was buried alive.

CHAPTER 1

A Bali hiatus

On a sunny Sunday in Perth, Western Australia on 4 November 2001, I received the customary call from Steve Bakovic (Bako):

'Wanna go to Freo for a coffee?'

This was Bako's usual catchcry, and my standard response was, 'Yeah, okay. What's Allen doing? Give him a call and I'll pick him up on the way through.'

Steve and Allen were childhood friends, and in the early part of the new millennium we usually hung out together on the cappuccino strip in our hometown of Fremantle, Western Australia. On this day, we sat outside Gino's Cafe, taking in the sights and talking about our lives and where we were heading. Steve, as usual, spoke about his ambitions of working in the airline industry, Allen talked about his interest in an acting career, whereas I was just enjoying my coffee. Inevitably the conversation turned to travel, and Allen and I started reminiscing about our trip to Bali in 1999. We spoke about the great time we'd had jetskiing and parasailing in Nusa Dua, visiting the Monkey Forest and having a splash at Waterbom Bali. We saw Bako's eyes light up as we laughed and joked about our antics two years earlier.

'Why don't we go to Bali again?' Allen said.

And even though Bako didn't need any further encouragement, I said, 'You'll never forget it.'

Little did I know that those four words would have such a literal meaning in the years to come. With that, our next overseas adventure was decided, and all we had to do was set a date.

Bako started sifting through his phone diary looking at possible dates. He came up with April 2002 as a suggested departure month. So, we left Fremantle that evening with smug smiles on our faces, believing that in less than five months' time, we would be drinking Bintang beside a pool and enjoying all that the island paradise has to offer.

In early January 2002, less than three months before our scheduled departure for Bali, I got a phone call at work. It was Bako. At that stage, I was employed as a fleet controller for Brambles Industrial Services, a global business that was involved in crane hire in Western Australia. My job was to schedule the heavy lift cranes for their day-to-day work. The job involved a lot of planning and taking phone calls from customers who needed a crane. The phone usually rang hot, so to get a call from someone who wasn't a client was a welcome relief amidst the office chaos.

'Hey, mate, I just realised April is school holidays, and the prices are a bit higher than usual; plus, there will be a lot of families hanging around with kids – might be a bit of a hassle getting a deckchair by the pool.'

This was how Bako started that conversation. After some deliberation, I agreed he was probably right and we should consider a change in date. After looking at our diaries, we decided that October looked like the best month. However, just as we were about to book, another setback arose. Allen threw a spanner in the works by deciding he wasn't going. The dynamics of our planned trip had changed, and we needed to reconsider our Bali holiday.

But Allen's change of heart wasn't to be the only setback.

CHAPTER 2

Family crisis

I'd moved out of my parents' home after buying my first house in February 2002. Late March 2002, I was outside doing some gardening when I got a call from my older brother, Glen.

'What are you doing? Come up to Mum's,' he said in a rather serious and to-the-point tone.

Immediately, I knew something wasn't right, so I quickly changed and drove up to the family home in Coogee. I walked in through the garage and as I entered the house, I saw my father sitting at the table with a sombre look on his face. Mum was standing at the kitchen sink, and Glen was sitting on the lounge. They all looked at me rather seriously. I initially thought I may have been in the proverbial for something I had done, then I noticed some X-ray papers on the kitchen table. I knew Dad had been experiencing some chest pain and had been to see his GP that day. I picked up the X-ray report and started reading. Tears welled in my eyes as I read that there was a shadow on Dad's lungs and he had been diagnosed with lung cancer. This was such a cruel blow to a man who had worked so hard all his life and was looking forward to retirement.

My dad, Pave (Paul), was the traditional family man. He escaped from the former Yugoslavia in 1965, and came to Australia looking for a better life. Dad was an avid smoker; he'd started early in his Navy days and enjoyed having a regular puff. As a youngster, I had always warned Dad about the dangers of smoking; however, he would always brush off my concerns with a wry smile.

The family was shell-shocked and couldn't believe the bad news. Of course, we assured Dad that we would offer all the support he needed to confront the challenge he had to face. Unfortunately, the cancer was a small-cell, fast-growing cancer, which had moved into his liver as well as his lungs. Despite attempts to kill it off with chemotherapy, his health quickly deteriorated and he passed away at the age of 61, on 22 May 2002, a mere eight weeks after being diagnosed with the illness. The sudden death of a beloved father and husband was a cruel blow to our family unit and made me realise just how fragile human life can be.

In the months that followed, we offered our mother all the support and love we could muster to help her deal with the sudden loss of her husband of 36 years.

The question of Bali still played on my mind, and I was faced with a dilemma as to whether I should go. I finally came to the conclusion that my father would have wanted me to get on with my life after his death, and that he would be in heaven keeping a watchful eye on us all as we moved on in our lives. So, we booked our departure for 11 October 2002, meaning I would celebrate my twenty-sixth birthday, on 14 October, in Bali.

Little did we know that others were also making plans – sinister ones – that would gate crash my celebration.

At that stage of my life, I was young and fit and played a lot of sport. On Tuesday nights, I had outdoor soccer training; Thursday

nights it was indoor soccer; Saturday mornings, Karate; and Sunday afternoons, a full game of outdoor soccer.

In the week beginning 7 October, indoor soccer was the highlight, as we had worked our way up to the Grand Final. After years of trying, and often making the Grand Final, we had never managed to win the competition. This time we were determined to make amends for previous losses. The final was on 10 October, just one day before my departure for Bali. It was a hard-fought game with both teams giving it their all, but we managed to hold on for a well-deserved win.

This was the perfect start to my holiday: a Grand Final win on the eve of seven days of sun, beer and relaxation in Bali.

CHAPTER 3

Sun, beer and relaxation

In the days prior to my departure, I chatted with my workplace manager about my impending trip to Bali. He was a veteran of many Bali holidays and told me a few stories of how one of his trips to the island had almost turned sour. He explained how he and his cousins had been on the dance floor, when all of a sudden glass started to rain down on them. The people standing on the upper level had started throwing glass bottles at them for no reason, and he and his cousins were lucky to escape injury. Perhaps this should have been the first warning that something might not be quite right about visiting Bali. Despite this, a holiday birthday in Bali sounded exciting and different from the usual fare.

The flight to Bali took three-and-a-half hours, a short haul compared with the long trips I had taken to Europe back in 1994 and 1997. So, it wasn't long before we were on our way to our hotel, Troppo Zone. It was located in the heart of Kuta, just a stone's throw from Paddy's Bar and the Sari Club. We shared our transport to the hotel with four other Western Australians, who were on their first trip to Bali. As we rode to the hotel, weaving through the narrow laneways, we discussed some of the things to do in Bali, and of our first impressions of the island.

We arrived at the hotel about 10pm on 11 October, dropped off our bags in our rooms and headed down to Paddy's Bar to get a 'feel' for the place. Whilst in Paddy's Bar that night, I noticed the ambience was somewhat different to what I had encountered on my previous trip in 1999. The number of Australians was down on previous years, and there were a lot of locals in the bar, mostly dressed in black clothing. It were as if the underworld had converged on Paddy's, and I felt somewhat uncomfortable about the place. My fears were further compounded after speaking with a local lady, who said to me:

'We go to another bar, this bar no good'.

Perhaps I should have seen this as the second warning that something wasn't right in Bali. Nevertheless, we stayed on at Paddy's a bit longer, and after finishing off a couple of pints we decided to call it a night and headed back to the hotel.

CHAPTER 4

The unexpected

After a good night's rest, we decided that we would spend the Saturday lazing around the pool, getting to know our fellow hotel guests. As it turned out, the four people we shared a cab with were staying at Troppo Zone as well, in the same part of the hotel. So, we caught up with them that afternoon around the pool area. For most of that afternoon, I lazed on an inflatable bed like a whale frolicking in the ocean, glad to be out in the warm sun and away from work for the week. Unfortunately, I paid the price for my relaxation, neglecting to slap on some sun cream, which resulted in some sunburn.

At about the same time, the terrorist network Jemaah Islamiyah was in its final stages of preparing their deadly attack. Having leased a safe house a few kilometres away from Kuta, the terrorists had spent the afternoon loading their van with explosives.

Later that afternoon, we attended 'Happy Hour' at the hotel bar with our fellow West Aussies and then had dinner at the hotel restaurant before returning to the bar for some further drinks. It wasn't long before I started feeling the effects of the local Bintang brew, and my sunburn was starting to sting. I decided to head back to my room to put some moisturiser on the sunburn. The others had decided they would check out the local club scene and headed off to the Sari Club, which was just up the road.

As I walked to my room, I stopped off at the toilet block near the entrance to the hotel and, whilst there, I remember experiencing a strange sensation. I had this image filter through my head of the toilet walls closing in on me, as if I were trapped inside the cubicle and couldn't get out. I shrugged off this sensation as the effects of the alcohol. Just outside the toilet block I bumped into Ryan, one of the four West Aussies.

'You coming down to the Sari?' he asked.

I stopped for a second and thought about it. In hindsight, I should have called it a night and headed back to my room, but I was in Bali and when you're in Bali, you don't go to bed at 9pm, so I agreed and off we went down the road towards the Sari.

Meanwhile at the hotel bar, Bako had struck up conversation with a Canadian girl, Deanna Thompson, who was also on holiday in Bali. They had gone back to her room with some others for a smoke before they were to come out.

The Sari Club was only about half-full when we got there at 9:15pm. There was still plenty of room to walk around freely, which was unusual for that club. The Sari was one of the most popular clubs on the Legian strip. It was made up of some thatched-roof cabana bars, joined together with a red-brick walkway with open areas around the club. There were two dance floors: one in the middle of the club next to a bar area, and another at the rear of the club.

Ryan and I caught up with Dave, who was standing on the edge of the middle dance floor, watching two girls dance. I ordered a round of Bintangs from the bar, and we stood there for about half an hour listening to the music. It was a typical Balinese night, humid with not a whiff of breeze about, conditions ripe for drinking and partying.

After about 45 minutes, the club started to fill up fairly quickly and before long there were people everywhere, laughing, dancing, drinking and generally having a good time. I had about a quarter of a Bintang left when I decided to head back to see where Bako was at, and if he was coming out. On my way out of the club, I sat down at the rear of the cabana bar about 10 metres from the exit, to finish off my Bintang. Whilst sitting there, I struck up conversation with two Australian girls, who were also on holiday in Bali. We spoke about our work lives and what had brought us to Bali, and after chewing the fat with them for a short time, I was about to excuse myself when all of a sudden, an almighty bang resounded from down the road.

I was sitting on a stool at the bar facing south towards Paddy's, which was 100 metres down the road, so immediately I looked towards the bar and I could see a huge mushroom cloud of black smoke rising from the roof of Paddy's.

I heard someone yell out, 'What the hell was that?'

Whilst the eyes of everyone in the front part of the Sari Club were firmly fixed on the scene down at Paddy's, my attention was drawn to the front door of the Sari, where I noticed an argument developing between the bouncers and someone else. Suddenly, I noticed two of the bouncers pull out the long dagger-like knives they kept tucked into brown leather holders strapped to their thighs.

At that stage, no-one inside the club had any idea there was a car bomb parked out the front of the Sari Club – and it was about to explode.

CHAPTER 5

Divine intervention

My recollection of the moments that followed are still somewhat blurred. Moments after I had watched the interaction at the entrance to the Sari, a van packed with explosives was detonated. The next thing I recall was waking up, lying on my back, buried under the thatched roof and timber that had been the cabana bar just seconds earlier. As I lay in the rubble of the Sari Club, dazed, confused and disorientated, I realised something terrible had occurred. Visions of firefighters with breathing apparatus sifted through my mind, and I had to make a split-second decision:

Do I lie here and wait for help to arrive, or do I try to get up and make my own way out?

I decided to take the latter option. In hindsight it was a decision that saved my life. I slowly began to lift the burning timbers off my body; some of them were long and heavy, and all I could do was push them off. But a sense of urgency gripped me as I realised I was burning alive. It didn't take long to clear the timbers and, like a phoenix rising from the ashes, I mustered all my strength and rose to my feet – this was the very beginning of my fight for survival.

As I looked around, the scene was very confronting. A complete change from what I had been experiencing just moments earlier. The dance floor, the people, the music, the girls I had been talking to, had all disappeared. All I could see was complete devastation. It were as if someone had driven a bulldozer through the club and levelled everything. To make things worse, there was fire everywhere. As I sought a way out of the club, or what was left of it, I looked to my left and on about a 45-degree angle I saw an extremely bright light, a white glow, hovering over an opening in a wall that had been blown out by the explosion. Instinctively, I started walking towards the hole, but with every step I took, my feet sank deeper into the debris-littered floor of the Sari. My heart started to beat faster; it felt as though the Sari was trying to swallow me. But guided by the glowing light, I made it to the hole in the wall and escaped the spreading inferno.

There is no feasible explanation for the glowing light I saw on that fateful night. The car bomb had knocked out the electricity grid in Kuta, and the only light on the streets was from the fires, which were starting to engulf Paddy's Bar and the Sari Club. Although we know evil was present on that terrible night, to this day, I truly believe that God was there also.

CHAPTER 6

Good deeds by good men

*'The only thing necessary for the triumph of evil
is for good men to do nothing.'*

- (attributed to) Edmund Burke -

Back at Troppo Zone, Bako received the fright of his life. He was sitting in Deanna's hotel room, chain smoking with a few others, when the windows of the room blew out as the explosive wave swept through the grounds of the hotel. His hands started to shake and he knew something was very wrong. The group huddled together in the middle of the room, some of the girls started to scream and cry, whilst chaos and panic reigned outside the two clubs.

As I made my way out of the Sari Club, clutching my badly injured left arm, I walked alongside a wall, and for a while I couldn't see anyone. I was starting to wonder if I had made the right decision. I was in severe pain and felt exhausted. Smoke from the fires had filled my lungs and I could walk no longer, so I simply collapsed against the wall. To the left of me, a young Asian girl was wailing in pain. She, too, was overcome by the smoke and as I gasped for breath, I asked her if she was okay.

She screamed, 'No!'

As I lay there slumped against the wall feeling helpless, I began to say my prayers. I'm not sure how long I lay there, but as I looked over to my right in the distance, I could see massive pillars of black smoke billowing from the rear of the Sari Club and I could hear a lot of shouting and screaming. I found out later that people were trapped at the rear of the club due to the lack of fire escapes, and some had to scale high walls to escape the inferno that had engulfed the Sari.

After getting my breath back, I also started to shout. This was the first time in my life that I felt completely helpless and in need of assistance. So, I shouted, 'Help! Help! Help!' as loud as I could. After yelling for a while, all hope seemed lost, when suddenly out of nowhere a Balinese man came running along carrying a metal sign, similar to a 'For Sale' sign for a house. I looked him squarely in the eyes and he gestured for me to get onto the makeshift stretcher. My prayers, and screams, for help had been answered, and as I wriggled myself onto the makeshift stretcher, staring up at the darkened sky, I said, 'Thank you, God'.

Soon after, other 'first responders' arrived and helped carry me away from the area. I never found out who these Balinese men were, but I am truly grateful for their heroics on that fateful night. Their good deeds helped restore my faith in humanity.

CHAPTER 7

The ute ride to hospital

As frantic calls were being made to Balinese Emergency Services and people started to grasp what had occurred, Australian doctors who happened to be on holiday in Bali at the time, set up a triage area outside the Bali cottages. This was a short distance up the same alley that the Troppo Zone hotel was located. It was here that my saviours had dropped me off, and it was here that Bako found me.

As I lay there on the bitumen, slipping in and out of consciousness, I heard someone yelling, 'Antony! Antony!'

It was a voice in the distance, but a recognisable one. I shouted back, 'I'm here, over here.'

'Where?' Bako called.

'Here!' I called back.

The area was full of casualties, and I was not easy to spot amidst the carnage of bodies but eventually, Bako found me.

His first words were, 'Are you all right?'

'No,' I shouted. 'I need water, please get me some water.'

His voice quivered as he said, 'Yeah, okay. I will go get some and come back soon. Hang in there.'

I was completely exhausted from my escape. My mouth was so dry and I was in desperate need of a drink. As I waited for Bako to come back, other people started to come past, asking me how I was. Then an Australian doctor came along and did a quick assessment of my injuries, checking my vitals.

He said, 'You'll be okay, just hang in there.'

This was reassuring, as I certainly didn't feel okay. But there were other people there who were in worse condition than me, so the doctors had to spread themselves thin and try to help as many people as they could.

It wasn't long before Bako came back with a bottle of water. I took some sips and this satisfied my thirst for the short term. Then I heard one of the doctors yelling out, 'One, two, three, four,' and so on; he was prioritising the order in which the injured should be evacuated from the area, with the worst going out first. I was number four on the list, but we had no idea how long this was going to take. The bomb had caused enormous damage on the Legian strip, which was a one-way road, so trying to get ambulances in and out was impossible, and with the number of casualties there certainly weren't going to be enough ambulances.

So, it was up to the good-hearted Balinese folk, who had excellent knowledge of all the backstreets, to ferry the injured to hospitals such as Sanglah, using any means possible. As I lay on the bitumen waiting for my number to come up, I was suddenly escalated to the top of the list. Bako was surprised but relieved that I was finally being taken to hospital, as he helped stretcher me onto the back of a ute.

The trip to the hospital was very painful, whilst Bako stood at the top end of the ute holding my head up and keeping my airway open, the burns to my body were starting to hurt. What made things worse was that every time the ute ran over a pothole, it felt as though I was being stabbed in the back, the pain reverberating throughout my entire body.

CHAPTER 8

The birthday I don't remember

Although the trip to hospital was painful, a stroke of luck saw me taken to the Kasih Ibu hospital in Jimbaran, as opposed to the main hospital Sanglah, which was struggling to cope with the mass casualties turning up on its doorstep. It is believed up to 450 people turned up at the hospital seeking help.

On arrival, I recall being offloaded from the ute and stretchered down a steep embankment to the doors of the clinic. But in their zest to get me to the clinic, the guys at the front of the stretcher were walking too fast, and the two guys at the back were struggling to keep up. I vividly recall Bako shouting, 'Hey, hey, slow down or I'll knock you out.' (Talk about leadership in a critical situation).

With Bako at six foot four, the Balinese took his threat seriously and slowed down, keeping me from falling off the stretcher. It wasn't until they put me down at the doors of the hospital that I realised just how bad I must have looked. By that stage, a crowd of onlookers was gathering outside the hospital. As I looked up, I saw a bunch of local women staring down at me. Their hands covered their mouths with a total look of shock and disbelief in their eyes.

My memory of the next 24 hours at the Kasih Ibu hospital is somewhat vague, as I was sedated for most of my time there. But according to reliable sources, I was operated on by the doctors in what they called a 'clean-up operation'. Apparently, I had also made a phone call home; however, I have no recollection of this call.

The next thing I remember was waking up inside a van. As I came out of sedation, all I could hear was the driver and his passenger talking in their native Bahasa language. I didn't know who they were or where they were taking me. For all I knew, I could have been in a hearse on the way to my own funeral. It turned out they were taking me to Denpasar airport for a medical evacuation.

The Australian Government, led by Prime Minister John Howard, had organised an aeromedical evacuation of all injured people who needed further treatment. Upon getting the go-ahead, the Royal Australian Airforce (RAAF) sent six of its C130J Hercules planes to Bali's Denpasar airport, loaded with medical teams and supplies. They set up a triage area in one of the hangars, where they assessed patients as they were brought in. Those who were critical were sent out first to the Royal Darwin Hospital in the Northern Territory.

To see the RAAF C130J Hercules on the tarmac and know I was about to be loaded into it was a great relief. And when one of the female RAAF attendants reassured me, I had never felt so proud to be an Australian.

'It's okay, matey, it won't be long now,' she said.

My last memory of leaving Bali was hearing the roar of the propellers on the Hercules as it thundered down the runway and took off.

The trip to Darwin was a short flight of three hours. The Hercules was well-suited to the task as it could fly at low altitude, thus negating the effects of air pressure that would have caused more damage to the injured patients' hearing, which had already been damaged when the bombs went off. I arrived at the Royal Darwin Hospital in the early hours of 14 October, my twenty-sixth birthday; however, I have no recollection of my time there as I was under heavy sedation for the duration of my stay.

The aeromedical evacuation of injured Australians and injured people from other countries was the largest ever conducted by the RAAF since the end of the Vietnam War. 'Within 37 hours the RAAF would complete the evacuation of 66 Australians and others to hospitals in Australia'.[1]

In war and in peace, the RAAF has always provided Australians with the reassurance that they will do their country proud. We are forever grateful to the brave men and women of the RAAF, who answered the call of duty to help their compatriots in their hour of need.

[1]Howard, J. (2012). 'Weekend Insight - Bali 10 years on', *Sunday Times*, 7 October 2012.

CHAPTER 9

'We do not expect him to survive'

'When people have nothing else left, especially due to war and other distressing circumstances, they draw an inner strength. These are God-given gifts of life that we, as frail human beings, use at times to support the soul and to give us courage and hope to continue with life even when the powers of hell prevail against us.' [2]

- Simun 'Sam' Sardelic -

Back in Perth my brother, Glen, was out fishing on my boat when he received a phone call from his then wife, Katarina. Glen remembers the call vividly.

'A bomb has gone off in Bali; come home quickly,' she said.

Glen pulled up anchor, threw the throttle into forward and hastily made his way back to the boat ramp, so hastily that he slammed the boat into the pier on his way in.

Back home, news of my plight had quickly spread, and it wasn't long before the phone at home was ringing hot with people concerned

---

[2] Sardeli S (2004) *'One Eye Crying'*, Small Print, Mandurah.

about my welfare. One of those was family friend Vjera Zanetic, who had heard I had been transferred to the Royal Darwin Hospital. Vjera's brother, Simun (Sam) Sardelic (dec.), was holidaying in Darwin at the time, so she called Sam and informed him of the situation, and asked him to go to the hospital to see what he could find out. Sam obliged and caught a cab to the hospital, where he was confronted with one of the worst scenes he said he had ever witnessed.

Like my father, Paul, Sam had migrated from the former Yugoslavia in 1946. He had worked hard to make a living on the railways in the wheat belt, before turning his attention to a business career in retail, becoming a successful entrepreneur. He had felt the effects of hardship whilst growing up in his native country and had experienced the hard knocks in life, but nothing could have prepared him for the trauma of what he saw at Royal Darwin.

When he arrived at the hospital, Sam asked if he could see me but the nurse refused, saying that only the patient's immediate family could visit.

Sam in his infinite wisdom said, 'Yes, but I'm his uncle and I've flown up from Perth especially to see him.'

The nurse, who was too busy to check details, obliged and allowed Sam into the ICU to see me. Entering the ward, Sam was confronted with a scene of total carnage. There were patients lying everywhere, bloodied, bandaged, some on respirators, struggling to stay alive. Doctors and nurses were running around frantically tending to blaring alarms and struggling to keep on top of things. Sam was completely shocked by what he saw and likened it to a scene from a war movie. Reaching my bed, he could see that my condition was dire. I was under sedation, wrapped in bandages and hooked up to a respirator.

Being a straight talker, Sam asked the doctor, 'What are his chances?'

The doctor replied, 'We do not expect him to survive.'

Sam left Royal Darwin feeling so shocked by what he had seen that he couldn't remember which hotel he was staying at, so he just told the cab driver to drive around for a while until they came across it. After finally finding the hotel and regaining his composure, Sam called his sister and told her the bad news. Vjera couldn't bear to tell my mother Marija, so she just told her that I was being treated at the hospital.

CHAPTER 10

Anatomy of a burns injury

The skin is the largest organ in the human body and serves two main purposes. First, it regulates core body temperature through the retention of fluids and the control of evaporation, and second, it provides a barrier to infection. Severe burns are a life-altering event. They cause immediate and long-term trauma to mind and body, and are arguably the most painful, unique and complex injury a human can suffer.[3]

The severity of a burn is categorised into four distinct descriptions: superficial, for minor burns to the epidermis; partial; deep partial; and full thickness, which can go right through to the bone. Fluid loss starts immediately after the burn occurs, because heat damage increases the permeability of the capillaries, which means that plasma is able to leak out of the blood's circulation. This increase disrupts the normal exchange of blood plasma into the extracellular space at the site of injury, which results in rapid fluid loss. The greatest loss of plasma occurs in the first 12 hours after burn injury. The plasma loss then slowly decreases during the second 12 hours of the post-burn phase, although extensive leakage can continue for up to three days.

---

[3]Fiona Wood Foundation website, 'Our challenge', *https://www.fionawoodfoundation.com/what-we-do/ our-challenge*, accessed 11 May 2022.

Optimal fluid replacement during this period is essential to ensure cardiac output, renal and tissue perfusion.[4]

Without fluid, the blood pressure of a patient with serious burns falls, kidneys and other organs fail, and then, they die. Hence, fluid replacement is a vital aspect of the treatment for a serious burn injury patient.[5]

Doctors use the Parkland formula to work out how much fluid is required to replenish the body. This formula advocates the guideline for total volume of the first 24 hours of resuscitation at approximately 4 ml per kilogram of body weight per percentage burn of total body surface area (TBSA). Half the volume is given in the first eight hours post-burn, with the remaining volume delivered over 16 hours.[6]

However, attention must also be paid to urine output and the central venous pressure, to ensure the right amount of fluid is being infused, as too little fluid infusion leads to multi-organ failure, whilst too much fluid can lead to swelling and cell death.

Infection is a major complication of a burn injury. Dead skin must be removed as it is a fertile playground for bacteria. Infection is usually treated with antibiotics, but in some cases the accumulated bacteria can become resistant to antibiotics, which can cause many organs to stop working.

So, in layman's terms, anyone who suffers a significant burn injury and doesn't get urgent medical treatment will inevitably die. In my case, I was in a critical condition and in desperate need of specialist medical care.

---

[4]Williams, C. (2008). 'Parkland formula – fluid resuscitation in burns patients 1: Using formulas', *Nursing Times*, 104:14, 28–29.
[5]Noble, T. (2003). 'How dozens of lives were saved in the flight of Bali', *The Age*, 5 October 2003, *https://www.theage.com.au/national/how-dozens-of-lives-were-saved-in-the-flight-of-bali-20031005-gdwhbs.html*, accessed 11 October 2003.
[6]Williams, C. (2008). 'Parkland formula', op cit.

CHAPTER 11

Patient unknown - condition critical

In Darwin hospital, my injuries were assessed as being critical, with infection taking hold of my body, I became hyperkalemic with metabolic acidosis, meaning there was too much potassium and acid in my blood, and I was suffering from hypovolaemic shock. Hypovolaemic shock is an emergency condition in which severe blood and fluid loss make the heart unable to pump enough blood to the body.[7] This type of shock can cause many organs to stop working and whilst in Darwin, I suffered renal failure, a condition where the kidneys fail to adequately filter waste products from the blood. To make matters worse, I was also suffering acute traumatic coagulopathy, which relates to the blood being unable to clot and can result in excessive or prolonged bleeding of wounds.

My burns and lung damage were the main cause of concern for the doctors, so they decided to put me into a deep sleep known as an induced coma. The induced coma, created with the use of anaesthetics, shuts down the body's secondary functions such as movement and speech, but keeps the vital organs working. This enabled my body's

[7]MedlinePlus (n.d.). 'Shock', National Library of Medicine, *https://medlineplus.gov/shock.html*, accessed 11 May 2022.

energy to be directed where I needed it the most, giving me the best chance of survival. The doctors in Darwin did the best they could to treat me and inserted a breathing tube down my throat, which pushed oxygen into my lungs. This decreased the metabolic demands of breathing, meaning my body didn't have to work as hard. They also performed an escharotomy on my left arm to reduce the effects of the swelling. The swelling associated with a burn injury can act like a tourniquet, stopping blood flow to an area of the body. This procedure involved slicing through dead skin to relieve the pressure on the affected area and allowing the blood to flow. To help cleanse the toxins in my blood they connected me to a continuous veno-venous haemodialysis (CVVHD) machine, which filters toxins from the blood. The doctors also used IV clotting products to reduce the effect of the coagulopathy, along with inotropes to help my heart keep beating. Inotropes are a chemical agent that can alter the force of muscular contractions and are used in the management of various cardiovascular conditions.

At 1am on 15 October, I was airlifted to Royal Perth Hospital (RPH) by the Royal Flying Doctor Service (RFDS). Although I was heavily sedated, the attending doctor's notes reveal that it was far from an uneventful trip. At 4:20am, my heart rate increased rapidly and it started to go into overdrive, a condition known as ventricular tachycardia. It was at severe risk of overexertion, which can prove fatal, so the doctor on board had to do something urgently to bring it back under control. So he punched my chest with his fist, to try to jolt my heart back into a normal rhythm. Luckily, the technique, known as a precordial thump, worked and my heart rate returned to normal, but this was just the start of my woes.

On arrival in Perth at 8am on 15 October, I was admitted to the Intensive Care Unit (ICU) at RPH, a high-dependency unit for the sickest of the sick. The unit was overflowing, as RPH had been allocated 28 patients from Royal Darwin. Other people were sent to hospitals all over the country, including Brisbane, Sydney and Adelaide.

The burns unit at RPH, led by Professor (Prof.) Fiona Wood, was well aware of the carnage in Bali as, by chance, one of their own trainee surgeons, Dr Vijith Vijayasekaran, had been holidaying in Bali at the time of the bombings. Dr Vij, who had recently completed burn-surgery training in Perth, played a crucial role in assessing, stabilising and coordinating the care of Australian patients injured in the bombings, and relaying important medical information back to RPH.

'A bomb blast typically damages a human in four ways. First comes the blast pressure wave, which can rupture internal organs, typically damaging lungs, bowels and eardrums. Second comes the heat,' which can burn lungs as well as skin. Third comes shrapnel, which can cause cuts, amputations and puncture wounds. Finally, there are crush injuries from building collapse. In Bali, that collapse was accompanied by an intense fire'.[8]

Unfortunately for me, I copped the lot. Full thickness burns to 60 per cent of my body, shrapnel wounds to both legs, lung damage from heat and smoke inhalation, bilateral perforated eardrums, cerebral oedema (swelling on the brain), and the onset of severe infection known as sepsis.

There was also a lot of swelling to my body, and my head inflated like a blow fish to the point it was difficult to confirm a positive identification by name. When my brother, Glen, came to see me in the ICU, he literally couldn't recognise me, so it was up to my mother, Marija, to identify me by looking at my fingers. I guess only a mother can recognise her child by looking at their fingers.

---

[8]Noble, T. (2003). 'How dozens of lives were saved in the flight of Bali', *The Age*, 5 October 2003, *https://www.theage.com.au/national/how-dozens-of-lives-were-saved-in-the-flight-of-bali-20031005-gdwhbs. html*, accessed 11 October 2003.

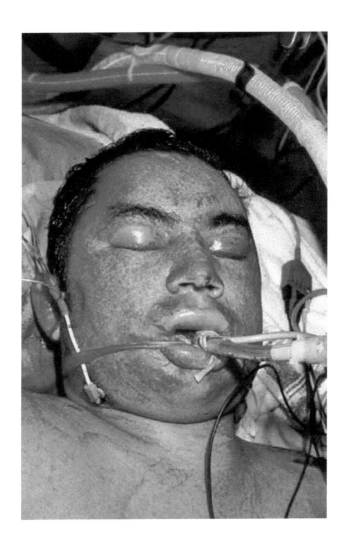

CHAPTER 12

Forty-four silent nights

The induced coma lasted for 44 days, during which time I had three lifesaving operations.

My first operation in Perth was conducted on 17 October 2002, and involved replacing the burnt skin on my arms with new skin, which had to be grafted from other areas of my body. However, the surgeons had a problem in that burns to 60 per cent of my body meant there was only 40 per cent of unburnt skin left to use for skin grafts. Generally, surgeons try to avoid using private parts of the body for skin grafts and take skin as close to the burn as possible to ensure it's a good match. To make 40 per cent of unburnt skin fit into 60 per cent, surgeons had to take skin from an unburnt part of the body and roll it through a machine, which puts tiny holes into the skin and turns it into a fine mesh. The meshed skin, known as a split skin graft, can then be stretched to cover an area twice the size of the initial graft. This meant surgeons now had close to 80 per cent of grafted skin to work with, more than enough to cover the 60 per cent required. Graft sites are considered the equivalent of a minor burn injury, so in one way they help to cover a burn injury, whilst at the same time becoming a wound themselves.

The magic of spray-on skin

In the mid-1990s, Prof. Fiona Wood and scientist Marie Stoner developed an innovative method of helping burnt skin to heal. They discovered that they could cultivate skin cells in a laboratory, and then spray these cells onto a graft site to help speed up the healing process. The spray-on skin, known as a cultured layer of cells, is applied over the tiny holes in the meshed graft and has the effect of promoting skin cell growth, whilst reducing the risk of infection.

However, the surgeons had yet another problem to contend with. The burns on my left arm were so severe that they had destroyed the inner layer of skin known as the dermis, which contains blood vessels, nerves, hair follicles and sweat glands. In a situation like this, surgeons can use a product called Integra, made from cow collagen, to trick skin cells into growing a new dermal layer. The Integra skin graft matrix is made up of several layers. The main layer functions as a scaffold. When placed on an appropriate wound, blood vessels and other cells start to migrate into the matrix. Then they start to build a new layer of dermis inside the matrix. Over a period of around a month, the collagen that makes up much of the matrix is slowly replaced with collagen made by the body. At the same time, new blood vessels grow into the matrix to supply the growing dermis.[9]

The Integra costs A$2500 for an A4-sized sheet and is imported from the United States in a glass of alcohol. Each sheet has to be rinsed for five to 10 minutes before it's applied, and then grafted skin from other parts of the body is carefully placed on top of the Integra to ensure there is a tight seal, preventing bacteria from getting in. Dressings are then applied to ensure it all remains in place, as any slight movement can undo the whole process. Nurses often write

---

[9]Boskey, E. (2020). Uses for Integra Skin Graft Substitute: Integra helps regrow skin after burns or reconstructive surgery, Verywell Health, 19 March 2020, *https://www.verywellhealth.com/integra-skin-graft-4796663*, accessed 23 May 2022.

'Integra. Do not move' on the dressings to warn other nursing staff of the caution that needs to be taken on parts of the body that have Integra on them.

During my first operation on 17 October, surgeons used Integra to create an artificial layer of dermal skin, stretching from my left hand all the way up to my left shoulder. This was a laborious process as it involved six nurses and two surgeons, working in a theatre heated to 36 degrees Celsius. The theatre is kept at this temperature to aid with blood flow in the patient's body, and although it's uncomfortable for staff to work in, it is vital for patient survival.

Despite the relative success of the first operation, from 23 October my condition began to deteriorate due to sepsis. 'Burn sepsis is one of the most common fatal burn injury complications...sepsis is a complication of severe infection. When the body is infected, it releases natural chemicals into the bloodstream. These chemicals are designed to fight off the infection. Sepsis develops when the body has an inflammatory response to its own infection-fighting chemicals'.[10]

---

[10]Burn Injury Guide, 'Burn Sepsis' (n.d.),
https://burninjuryguide.com/burn-recovery/burn-complications/burn-sepsis/, accessed 30 June 2022.

As a result, the patient may experience decreased blood flow to vital organs. 'If sepsis is left untreated, the patient may go into septic shock'.[11]

I had many bacteria in my body, including Fusarium solani, Bacillus cereus, Enterococcus, Candida, Enterobacter, Pseudomonas and multi-resistant Acinetobacter baumanii. Doctors used eleven types of antibiotics: Flucloxacillin, Gentamicin, Metronidazole, Tobramycin, Ciprofloxacin, Vancomycin, Meropenem, Teicoplanin, Moxifloxacin, Voriconazole and Contrimoxazole, in a concerted effort to kill every microbe known to man.[12]

The burns on my back had a bacterial infection called Pseudomonas aeruginosa. Pseudomonas is a type of bacterium (germ) that is commonly found in the environment, like in soil and in water,

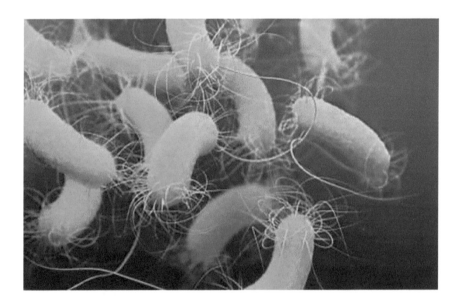

[11]Ibid.
[12]Wong, K (2002). *ICU Discharge Summary*, Royal Perth Hospital, 25 November 2002.

which can cause infections in the blood, lungs (pneumonia), or other parts of the body after surgery.[13]

Bacteria are constantly finding new ways to avoid the effects of the antibiotics used to treat the infections they cause. If they develop resistance to several types of antibiotics, they are classed as multidrug-resistant. The clouds of dust at the blast site, and the unclean water, meant that all the serious burn patients developed infections, some of which had never been seen before in Australia.

To make matters worse for me, the lack of food in my gut caused the good bacteria inside my stomach to seep through my gut lining and into my blood stream, meaning my own body was now attacking me as well. As my body temperature hovered around 40 degrees Celsius, nurses used small bags of ice cubes under my arm pits and knees to try to bring it down.

[13]Centre for Disease Control and Prevention (n.d.). 'Pseudomonas aeruginosa in Healthcare Settings', *https://www.cdc.gov/hai/organisms/pseudomonas.html*, accessed 23 May 2021.

CHAPTER 13

Dire straits

My sepsis became severe and eventually turned into septic shock, 'a condition characterized by a dramatic drop in blood pressure. This can lead to organ failure and death. Septic shock patients typically also experience symptoms such as difficulty breathing, abnormal heart function, abdominal pain, and confusion or disorientation'.[14] In septic shock, a person's blood pressure cannot be maintained by intravenous fluids alone, so inotropes were reintroduced to try to stabilise my heart. The doctors were dumbfounded; they were using the strongest antibiotics they had at their disposal, but my condition worsened by the hour.

Something had to be done, but an operation at this stage was a tough call to make as there was a good chance I could die on the operating table. In consultation with other senior doctors, and using all her years of clinical experience, Prof. Fiona Wood assessed the situation and made the call. Emergency surgery was to be performed as soon as possible.

---

[14]Burn Injury Guide, 'Burn Sepsis', op cit.

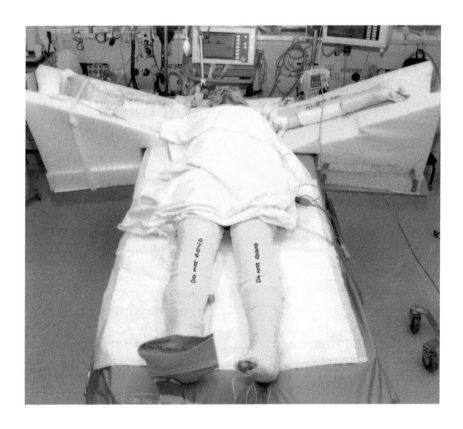

CHAPTER 14

A mother's plea

Prof. Fiona Wood is the Director of the Western Australia Burns Service and the Royal Perth Hospital burns unit at the time. She was well trained in dealing with significant burn injuries. By this stage, two patients from the bombings had already died, and with my life hanging in the balance, Prof. Wood conducted the surgery.

Prior to going into theatre, Prof. Wood told my family to spend as much time as they wanted with me, as it could be the last time they would see me alive. It was at this stage my mother made an impassioned plea to Prof. Wood.

She said, 'Fiona, I lost my husband six months ago to cancer. Please don't let me lose my son.'

Prof. Wood, a mother of six children, was visibly moved by this emotional plea and promised to do all she could to save my life.

The operation was carried out on the evening of 24 October. My family decided to go home and wait for news of my fate, rather than hang around the hospital corridors. As word spread of my plight, a small group of extended family and friends gathered at the family home, waiting for news as it developed.

The surgery commenced at 6:30pm and required two plastic and reconstructive surgeons, due to the size of the surgery. As a result of gut failure and rising lactate levels (a gauge of septic shock), surgeons were concerned I had a lack of blood flow to the bowel (ischaemia) so a laparotomy was carried out by plastic and reconstructive surgeon Dr Mark Duncan-Smith. A laparotomy is a surgical procedure involving a large incision through the abdominal wall to gain access into the abdominal cavity.[15] Dr Duncan-Smith found a haematoma, which is a localised swelling that is filled with blood caused by a break in the wall of a blood vessel – common in blast injuries. Once this was drained, he checked my gall bladder, looking for signs of infection. After stapling my stomach back together it was time to reconstruct my badly burnt back.

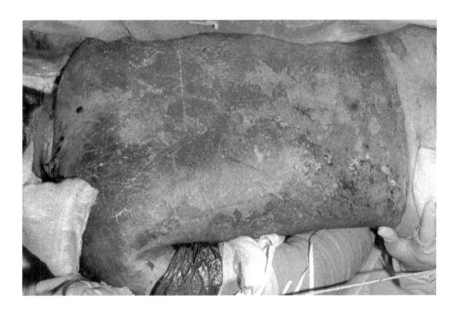

[15]Clinical Trials.gov (n.d.). 'Treatment for Malignant Ovarian Cancer: Laparoscopy vs Laparotomy', U.S. National Library of Medicine, *https://clinicaltrials.gov/ct2/show/NCT02686463*, accessed 31 May 2022.

CHAPTER 15

'Cometh the hour, cometh the woman'

In tight games of football, veteran English football commentator Martin Tyler would cite the old English proverb 'Cometh the hour, cometh the man', to describe a player who would rise to the occasion and produce a special performance to lift his team to victory. In my situation it was a case of 'Cometh the hour, cometh the woman', as Prof. Wood began the arduous process of rebuilding my burnt back. First, it was a case of stripping away all the burnt skin in a process called debridement, which exposes the raw flesh underneath. Skin grafts were then taken from other parts of my body to use as new skin. Skin cells cultivated and grown from my previous operations were now ready to use as spray-on skin. It was a race against time as Prof. Wood worked feverishly to repair the damage. She later said that she slapped on the skin grafts as quickly as possible to give me the best chance of survival. Several pints of fresh, warm blood were infused to help the new skin settle and, once the skin grafts were in place, spray-on-skin was used to seal the grafts.

A tracheostomy was also performed, which consisted of making an incision on the front (anterior) aspect of my neck and opening a direct airway through an incision in my windpipe (trachea). A tracheostomy tube was then inserted, which allowed me to breathe without the use of my nose or mouth. In the context of my precarious situation, this was important as it reduced the risk of infection from having a tube going down my throat.

By 1:00am, my fate was sealed; I had survived the emergency surgery and was wheeled back to the intensive care unit for around-the-clock monitoring. Back home my family, who were almost dying from anxiety, received the call they had long been waiting for. The nurse told them I had pulled through and was recovering in the ICU. I'm told a loud cheer rang through the household, and they went to bed early that morning with a sense of relief.

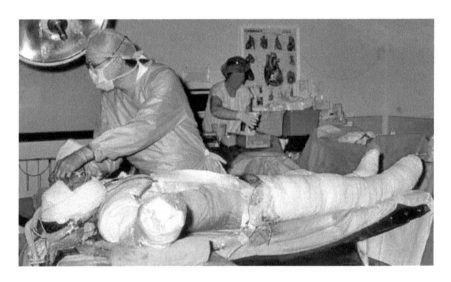

In the days that followed, my condition gradually improved. By 1 November, my gut was absorbing feeds and my renal function was good. But I was continuing to experience high fevers of up to 41 degrees Celsius, and I was encephalopathic. The hallmark of encephalopathy is an altered mental state resulting in agitation and jactitation, meaning a restless tossing and turning of the body, and often an involuntary spasm of a limb or muscle.

Nevertheless, I continued to improve and by 7 November, all antibiotics were ceased; however, my confused and agitated state was making it difficult for the nurses. To control my agitation and keep me calm during daily dressing changes, doctors had me on a cocktail of Ketamine, Fentanyl, Haloperidol, Diazepam, Clonidine, Morphine elixir and sublingual Midazolam/Ketamine. However, on one occasion I woke up during the dressing change, and it felt like someone was prodding me with a cattle prod. Every time they took off a dressing, the pulsating pain reverberated throughout my entire body to the point where this was the only time I wished I were dead.

My healing continued and on 14 November, I was taken to the operating theatre again for split skin grafts and spray-on skin to be applied to my arms, legs and laparotomy wound. In the days that followed, the wounds were healing well, and the daily dressing changes were keeping the dreaded infection away. But just when I thought I was out of the woods, on 23 November I contracted Varicella zoster virus (chickenpox) – as if to rub salt into my wounds. This was treated with a medicine called Valacyclovir, to nip it in the bud before it took hold.

On 25 November my sedation was lifted, I was decannulated and weaned off the ventilator and breathing through a T-piece. My pain medication was adjusted to control the encephalopathy, which was by now largely resolved.

I didn't know at the time but in the room next door, another battle for life was being played out. Simone Hanley had been in the Sari Club when the bomb went off and, like me, she was airlifted out to Perth. Her family had flown over from Sydney to keep vigil over their daughter. I was told later that as I came out of my sedation, Mary Jane Hanley and her sister, Kristine, were looking through the internal window to my room when Mary Jane quipped that I looked like a 'daddy-long-legs' spider with my hands and legs flapping all over the place. She told her sister that the nurses were having a hard time subduing me. At that stage they instinctively knew I would survive; but Simone's life still hung in the balance.

CHAPTER 16

Goodbye ICU

When I woke from my 44-day coma, I was greeted by my brother, who had been eagerly awaiting my awakening. He asked me if I knew where I was, and I told him I was in hospital. He was glad that I was aware of my surroundings, as it showed that my brain was functioning normally. It felt good to be awake again, but I was hot; in fact, it felt like I had a pot-belly stove boiling away in the pit of my stomach. The pulsating heat felt like it was burning my oesophagus. The only way to soothe this sensation was with ice cubes. In the proceeding days, I looked forward to my brother's twice-daily visits, as he would always bring a cup of ice cubes with him. He was under strict instruction to only give me a maximum of six ice cubes, as there was a risk water could get into my lungs, which could cause pneumonia. Before he fed me the ice cubes, he would ask me to wink three times and nudge once. Initially, I thought this was some sort of stupid game he had come up with, and I was getting rather annoyed by it all. But it actually served a purpose, as it tested my responsiveness and ability to accept the ice in my mouth. As he fed the ice cubes to me one by one, I would crush them with my teeth and the ice would run down the back of my throat and into my gut, providing an unrivalled cooling sensation.

The ice cubes, the morning floss with a sweet tasting swab to clean my mouth out, along with visits from my family members, were the things I looked forward to the most during my prolonged stay in the ICU. You can never underestimate the effect a burn injury has on your family, as they suffer the anguish and torment of not knowing if you will pull through. They can only assume the pain you are feeling and often they fear the worst, so it was certainly a difficult time for all involved. But my family never lost hope during my battle for survival. They spent many hours beside my bed, praying for me. In fact, there were prayer gatherings in churches throughout Australia and around the world for the survivors – and victims – of the bombings.

A memorable day for me was 6 December 2002 because I finally left the ICU. Being in the ICU was a strange experience, as I found myself hanging somewhere between life and death, at the mercy of God, not knowing which way the pendulum would swing. There was no concept of time or day, and everything became irrelevant apart from my health. To say the doctors and nurses had pulled out all stops to save my life would be an understatement. As the nurse started unravelling the myriad of tubes and cords from the machines that had kept me alive for the past 52 days, she explained that I was going up to the burns unit, to begin my physiotherapy and rehabilitation with senior physio Mr Dale Edgar. As my bed was wheeled out, a number of the medical staff came up and wished me well. It was a special moment for them, as they had fought a long and hard battle to keep me alive. Leaving ICU was a defining moment on my road to recovery.

CHAPTER 17

The burns unit

In the burns unit, I was deliberately allocated the bedroom directly in front of the nurses' station so they could keep a close eye on me. Once I had settled into my room, a male nurse came in and explained to me where I was and gave me a rundown of the hospital as part of my orientation. He explained what level of the hospital I was on and said that there were ocean views from the rooftop level. But this was cold comfort to me, as I could hardly move let alone get to the roof to enjoy ocean views. After spending 52 days in the ICU lying on my back, all my muscles had gone to sleep. To make matters worse, protein stores in my muscles had whittled away and my weight had plummeted to 58 kgs, down 20 kgs from my normal weight.

It is difficult to explain the sensation of a burn injury. The only thing that comes close is a prolonged bout of the influenza virus, where everything hurts and you feel as though you have had the life sucked out of you. Whilst the induced coma had given me the best chance of survival, it came at a price. I couldn't move anything: fingers, hands, arms, feet, legs, neck or back. In fact, I felt like a plank of wood lying helplessly in bed – the psychological impact of this was devastating. One minute I had been playing sport four times per week, and the next I didn't have the strength in my fingers to change channels with the remote control. This was the only time I cried during my entire hospital stay.

To help with my lack of strength, the nurses gave me a little bell to ring if I needed attention. But the only way I could use this was to physically knock it off the table with the back of my hand, and hope the nurses heard it as it dropped to the floor. On some occasions they heard it and on others they didn't, so quite often if I needed a drink or a change of linen, I would have to wait a while until they came in to do their observations.

The lack of control of my bowels was rather embarrassing, as I would quite often soil the bed, on some occasions two to three times per night. Although there were only two nurses on duty during the night, they would always come in to clean me up and change my bed linen, which I was always very grateful for. Urination was never an issue as I had a catheter inserted to drain the fluids from my bladder. However, the way I found out about the catheter was rather amusing. I had very little feeling below the waist and whenever the physios came in to get me up and out of bed, they would always strap this bag full of amber-coloured fluid to the side of their waist, and I couldn't figure out what it was. Then when I had my first shower in just over 52 days, I looked down between my legs and saw this thin tube coming out of the end of my penis. Although I was horrified, it all became clear to me.

CHAPTER 18

You have to be cruel to be kind

'A journey of a thousand miles begins with a single step.'

- Lao Tse -

The burns unit team worked by the motto 'You have to be cruel to be kind', as they knew from years of research and past experience that for a burn survivor to regain full movement, they need to start working the muscles and joints as soon as possible after the burn injury is sustained. In my case they did as much as they could whilst I was in the ICU, and I do recall being hydraulically lifted on a board to help me regain my vertical orientation. However, there is no substitute for physical exercise when it comes to burn rehabilitation, and the sooner a patient gets out of bed and starts walking, the better.

In my case that first walk was to come earlier than I expected; much earlier. It was late afternoon on my first day in the burns unit, when a tall gentleman wearing a green shirt and khaki-coloured shorts came in and introduced himself as Dale Edgar. Although he spoke with a calm demeanour, there was a sense of purpose in his voice. When he asked me if I was ready to go for a walk, I almost died; he was adamant I should get out of bed and go for a stroll. But he had it all planned beforehand, and before I could offer any resistance, he brought in a wheelchair and parked it a foot away from the bed. He whisked my legs over the side of the bed and asked me if I could get into the chair. But there was no chance I was going to be able to hoist myself into it. So, with the help of another physio, they heaved me into the chair and before I knew it, I was being wheeled away. The trip was a short one, just to my bedroom door, where another physio was waiting patiently.

Dale said, 'Okay, we are going to get you up, and you see that yellow door down there, do you reckon you could walk to that and back?'

The door was only five metres away, but as far as I was concerned, it may as well have been 50 metres away; there wasn't a hope in hell I was going to get there and back without suffering another coronary. But with the help of the three physios, one in front and one on each side, I got up from the wheelchair. They encouraged me to take my first step. I gingerly took a step with my right foot and then tried to do the same with my left, but it wouldn't move. My left knee had suffered a shrapnel injury from the explosion and Prof. Wood had to carry out a 'knee wash' to remove the shrapnel and accumulated bacteria. As a result, the tendon had grown back short and needed to be stretched out to enable the knee to bend, but it wasn't going to happen in a hurry, so to compensate I had to hook my left leg around by swinging the left side of my body. So, it was one step forward with my right leg then a hook around with the left to move forward. It was hard work, and I was grimacing with pain, but I was doing it. My legs felt like jelly and to make matters worse, due to medication I shook like a sieve, and there was nothing I could do to control it.

As I took a few more steps, I looked over at the nurses' station and a young nurse sitting at her desk looked back at me. She had tears running down her face before she quickly turned away. I thought to myself, geez I must really look like shit. Eventually, and with a lot of help from the physios, I did make it to the yellow door and back. But I was completely spent, so much so that upon returning to my bed it took me half an hour to regain my breath. These were the first steps I had taken in just over 52 days, and they had flattened me. So, as I lay on my bed staring up at the ceiling, it soon dawned on me that my rehabilitation was going to be a real test of strength and character.

There was more physiotherapy to come – lots more – in fact, the routine was a session in the morning from 9–10am, then an afternoon session from 5–6 pm. But on my second day in the burns unit there was an important task that needed to be done: my very first shower since arriving at RPH on 15 October 2002, 53 days earlier.

Whilst in the ICU, the nurses had only been able to hand wash me with wet cloths. So, to finally have a proper shower was a blessing, but this would not be the simple task that most people take for granted each day. Given I couldn't stand or walk on my own, it meant I had to be wheeled into the bathroom in a shower chair, and because I couldn't use my hands, it meant the nurses had to wash me down. My first shower was memorable, and as the nurses washed me down with chlorhexidine solution, I felt so refreshed that when the nurses went to turn the water off, I politely asked if I could stay under the water just a little bit longer.

They smiled and replied, 'Of course you can.'

Once I was out of the shower and back into bed, it was time for a visit from the doctor and for new dressings to be applied. This practice would turn into a regular routine for the next 30-odd days. Dressing changes were the last thing I looked forward to as the associated pain was excruciating. Morphine was the most effective pain relief available, and it could be administered in two ways, either through the intravenous drip or orally, as a liquid you drink. The intravenous method was better, as it meant I didn't have to taste the shit, which

I must say is the most foul-tasting medication I have ever taken. But even as it was injected, I could still feel the cold liquid making its way up my arm and into my body, like a worm wriggling its way through my veins. The morphine was usually provided half an hour before a dressing change, and if I had to take it orally, I would always have a glass of orange juice nearby to take away the taste somewhat. However, despite my dislike for this painkiller, it served its purpose well and dulled the pain associated with dressing changes.

I had heard stories of morphine changing people's personalities, and of some people experiencing hallucinations. The guy who was in the room down from me used to swear like a trooper, but all I ever experienced was seeing black stallions running around in my room. They would bolt in through the doors, do a couple laps of the room and then leave within seconds down the hallway to their next destination.

CHAPTER 19

A wicked and despicable act

'Australia has been affected very deeply, but the Australian spirit has not been broken. The Australian spirit will remain strong and free and open and tolerant.'

- John Howard -

Whilst I was in the ICU, I didn't really know what had occurred in Bali, apart from it being something terrible. It wasn't until I had settled into the burns unit that I started to get some exposure to the event. It was Glen who first explained to me what had happened; however, he was reluctant to provide too much detail for fear that it would affect me psychologically. Then when I started to watch the evening news, I discovered just how barbaric the attacks had been. That two bombs had ripped apart Paddy's Bar and demolished the Sari Club was common news around the world and the media had gone into a frenzy reporting the atrocity.

Three terrorists known as Ali Imron, Arnasan and Feri had driven a van packed with up to 1.2 tonnes of explosives made up of a mixture of potassium chlorate, aluminium powder, C4, RDX and other chemicals, to Kuta. As the van, driven by Ali Imron, arrived at an intersection in Kuta, Imron got out, leaving Arnasan to deliver the bomb. Imron's job was simply to make sure the other two terrorists got to Kuta. As the van then meandered its way down the four-kilometre-long main street of Kuta, known as Legian Road, it stopped to allow Feri, who had a custom-made bomb vest strapped to his chest, laden with plastic tubes of explosives attached to a detonation chord, to get out and walk towards Paddy's Bar. Feri walked into Paddy's unchecked by security and moved towards the back of the bar where the majority of people were. It was here that he pulled the detonation chord on his suicide vest, sending a mushroom cloud of smoke into the sky above Paddy's Bar.[16]

The van, by now parked at the front of the Sari Club, was detonated at precisely 11:08:31pm, causing a massive blast that shook the foundations of Kuta. 'There was an immediate, deafening roar, crimson and orange flames soared into the black sky. Bricks, timber, metal and glass mangled together – tossed into a furious jumble to all parts of the street...fire damage spread in a radius of 200 metres from the van, and the bomb left a crater four metres wide and 60 centimetres deep. Police verified a total of 58 damaged buildings, 19 ruptured cars and 32 destroyed motorbikes. Body parts were strewn all over the scene, found later on roofs and back yards streets away'.[17]

'The bomb was massive enough to set off the seismic equipment used to record earthquakes in Bali. The impact could have been far worse, up to 1.2 tonnes of explosives were packed into the bomb van but, because of the terrorists lack of experience, it only had an effective charge of about 300 kilograms. More than two thirds of the explosives burned, rather than boosting the blast'.[18] Heaven only knows how many more people would have died if not for the incompetence of the terrorists.

[16]Goodsir, D. 'The night terror touched our lives', op cit.
[17]Ibid.
[18]Forbes J, Silvester M (2003). 'How they got the bombers', *The Age*, 6 October 2003, *https://www.theage.com.au/national/how-they-got-the-bombers-20031006-gdwhid.html*, accessed 11 October 2003.

In the days that followed, Australian Prime Minister John Howard, described it as a 'wicked and despicable' act and said that no stone would be left unturned in capturing the terrorists and bringing them to justice.

CHAPTER 20

Capturing the terrorists

Within a week of the bombing, Indonesian President Megawati Soekarno-putri signed an agreement in Jakarta for a historic joint investigation into the bombing. On the Indonesian side, General Made Pastika was named as the Chief Investigator, which was seen as being beneficial as he had ties with senior members of the Australian Federal Police.

The investigation involved up to 120 Australian Police officers, who would be based in Bali. They came from all states and territories and included forensic officers, victim identification officers, detectives and undercover ASIO agents. These teams were backed up by 400 Australian Federal Police officers, and over 1000 state police back in Australia, making it the biggest police investigation in Australia's history.[19]

The investigators' first big break came when a night watchman of a small mosque two kilometres away reported seeing two men park a motorbike outside after the bombings. Explosive residue from the bike confirmed its link to the bomb site, and the bike was traced to a

---

[19]Ibid.

local dealership where it had been sold two days earlier. The salesman recalled the three men who had bought the bike, and within 24 hours, Victorian police face-fit experts produced three images of the men: Amrozi, Idris and Ali Imron. The images were broadcast on national TV and were so good that when Amrozi saw his face on TV, he went to the hairdresser twice to try to change his appearance.

Investigators knew the Sari Club bomb had gone off precisely at 11:08:31pm, as it had set off seismic equipment on the island. But they were not sure what had happened in Paddy's Bar. Suggestions that a suicide bomber had set off the blast were scoffed at by the Indonesians, but DNA evidence scraped off the ceiling at Paddy's Bar was matched to remains at the mortuary bearing all the hallmarks of a suicide bomber. The investigators knew it was a terrorist attack, but didn't know who had caused it. However, the Al-Qaeda network was on top of their list of suspects, due to their success in bringing down the World Trade Centre, aka the Twin Towers, in New York, some 12 months earlier. Investigators analysed the Sari bomb scene and discovered that potassium chlorate was the main ingredient in the bomb. Undercover ASIO agents suggested this could have been purchased by individuals connected to the radical Jemaah Islamiyah network, a subsidiary of the Al-Qaeda network. Their hunch proved correct, but it was a twist of fate that allowed them to discover who was behind this deadly attack.

The investigators knew a van had been parked outside the Sari Club, but they had no evidence linking it to any of the three identified men until they took a closer look at a steel identification plate on the van. The culprits had filed away the engine and chassis numbers, but unbeknown to them, beneath a welded plate there was another number, which had been used to register the vehicle as a bus some 15 years earlier. The police got the big break they had been waiting for when they were able to trace that number to the original owner, then track the vehicle to a village on Java, where the last registered buyer said he had sold it to Amrozi. The police team pounced and arrested Amrozi in Java. Within hours of his arrest, he made a partial confession to police and provided vital information about who had assisted him in the bombing and what had occurred. Physical evidence in the form of bags of potassium chlorate were taken from his premises. The pieces were starting to fall into place and after more interrogation, Amrozi identified Imam Samudra as the leader of the terrorist plot.

Samudra had already been on ASIO's radar as he was behind a number of religious bombings in Indonesia. After scouring the countryside for weeks looking for Samudra, police got their break when the tracking of his mobile and internet use directed them to the port of Merak, where he had been planning to board a ferry to Malaysia. Samudra was promptly arrested and hauled away for questioning. The police had finally got their main man, and it wasn't long before they arrested some of the other key players in the planning and execution of South-East Asia's worst terrorist bombing.[20]

After a lengthy and dramatic trial, all three men: Amrozi – dubbed the 'smiling assassin' because of his frivolity in openly confessing to the bombings, Imam Samudra and Ali Imron were all sentenced to death by firing squad for their roles in planning the bombings.

Other players were given lengthy prison sentences and police had gathered vital information on the Jemaah Islamiyah terrorist network, enabling them to conduct successful raids on the terrorists' activities that subsequently thwarted other planned bombings since their ruthless attack on 12 October 2002. However, the challenge for police and intelligence agencies is that they have to get it right 100 per cent of the time to prevent a terrorist attack. Whereas the terrorists only have to get it right once to leave a bloody mark on their intended targets. This was later proven when on 1 October 2005, suicide

---

[20]Ibid.

bombers struck at the heart of Bali again, killing 20 people, including four Australians, in a series of coordinated bombings.

Terrorism is a real and constant threat in many parts of the world. The London bombings in 2006, the Madrid train bombings in 2008, the Boston marathon bombings in 2013, and the attacks in France and Thailand in 2016, prove that this is the case. With Allied troops pulling out of Afghanistan in 2021, after a 20-year war with the Taliban, the threat of terror has not subsided.

CHAPTER 21

Recovery

'Where there is life, there is hope.'

- Stephen Hawking - [21]

'A scar is collagen-rich skin formed after the process of wound healing, which differs from normal skin. Scarring occurs in cases where there is repair of skin damage, but the skin fails to regenerate the original skin structure. Fibroblasts generate scar tissue in the form of collagen, and the bulk of repair is due to the basket-weave pattern generated by collagen fibres and does not result in regeneration of the typical cellular structure of skin. Instead, the tissue is fibrous in nature and does not allow for the regeneration of accessory structures such as hair follicles, sweat glands or sebaceous glands'.[22]

The major issue with burn scarring is not so much the aesthetic image, but rather the restriction in movement you get in a joint when

---

[21]Ashok, I. (2017). '"Where there is life there is hope" – Stephen Hawking shares incredibly inspiring life lessons', *International Business Times*, 23 November 2017, *https://www.ibtimes.co.uk/where-there-life-there-hope-stephen-hawking-shares-incredibly-inspiring-life-lessons-1648595*, accessed 29 June 2022.
[22]Course Hero (n.d.). 'Anatomy and Physiology I, Module 6: The Integumentary System Diseases, Disorders, and Injuries' *https://www.coursehero.com/study-guides/austincc-ap1/diseases-disorders-and-injuries-of-the-integumentary-system/*, accessed 11 May 2022.

the scar covers areas such as your armpits, affecting the shoulder joint, or around your fingers. The only way to prevent this restriction is to move the joint as much as possible whilst it is healing; otherwise, it will require surgical intervention. The physiotherapists spent a lot of time bending my fingers, wrists and elbows in every conceivable way to try to get them moving, and the day I touched my nose with my thumb was memorable, as it had taken three weeks of twice-daily physio to get to this point.

Even though I could touch my nose, I still had to learn how to stand on my own two feet and walk again, which was far from easy as my balance had been distorted from permanent damage to the area containing fluid surrounding my left cochlear. Every time I tried to stand on my own, I felt as though I was going to tip over and fall on my head, hence it took weeks of practice and vertical orientation to finally be able to walk with the assistance of a walking stick. To make walking even more difficult, I had to wear a pair of 'moon boots' day and night. These plaster boots were designed to keep my ankle joints at 90 degrees so my feet didn't flop. Coupled with this, I had to wear a pressure garment called 'second skin' for almost 12 months, which is similar to a wetsuit and is designed to apply constant pressure to the skin to keep the developing scarring as flat as possible. The garment became very hot in the summer months and the skin underneath was itchy, making it uncomfortable to wear. I also had an acrylic mask that I wore during the day and a fabric mask for night-time, so I looked like Spiderman in a beige-coloured suit.

The physios and occupational therapists on the ward were worth their weight in gold as they continually pushed me to my maximum every day. The outcome you get from a burn injury is dependent on the amount of effort you put in, and I was determined to get the best result possible. So much so that the nurses called me a 'freak', as I was the only burn patient on the ward who would do my bed exercises when the physios weren't around. The nurses themselves weren't afraid to offer words of motivation, and quite often when I tried to take an afternoon kip, head nurse Sheila would come marching into my room to tell me off.

'Antony, we sleep during the night and work during the day...do your bed exercises,' was one of the things I remember her telling me.

The term 'move it or lose it' also rang in my head like a worn-out Gangnam song. I was determined to regain full movement in all parts of my body. Special thanks go to nurses Sheila, Carol, Lyn, Anna and Georgie for their continuous encouragement.

I always knew when Dale Edgar was on the ward, as he kept a set of keys hanging off his belt, and as soon as he came through the second door of the burns unit, I'd hear the keys rattle, sending a ringing vibration down the corridor and down the spine of every patient on the ward. Most of the physios went easy on me and I was able to talk my way out of the most demanding exercises, but there was no easy way out with Dale. He had an imposing stature and wouldn't take no for an answer, until you had almost collapsed from exhaustion.

In one particular session Dale wanted me to get down onto my knees, but my quadricep muscles and hamstrings were as taut as guitar strings, which made bending my knees extremely difficult and painful. For a long time, I'd had a severe pain in my left knee just below the kneecap, because the tendon had grown back short, and it needed to be stretched out to enable the knee to bend. The pain was restricting my movement and whenever I walked, I continued my habit of swinging my left leg across rather than bending the knee, just to avoid further pain. Dale knew that I needed to start bending my knees if I was to stretch the tendons, especially the left one. The pain was intense, and I argued vehemently whilst writhing in pain, but Dale was adamant I should kneel so the muscles could stretch out. In the end I fell over sideways, and Dale realised it wasn't going to happen that day.

However, Dale knew that failure is no match for perseverance. Within a few days, I was back down in the gym for another attempt. On this occasion, Dale had brought a couple of other physios along to help, and the extra hands worked well. As they lowered me down, I was able to get onto my knees for the first time since arriving at RPH. It was painful, but psychologically it was a big win, as it showed I could break through the pain barrier and stretch out the tightest of muscles. This forceful approach to my physiotherapy is the reason I have such great movement in my body today, and I thank all the physios and occupational therapists who helped me out. In particular, Dale, Nick, Michelle, Vidja, Dominie, David, Megan and Amanda, for their tireless work in helping me regain my movement. Dale went on to earn his doctorate in physiotherapy and is an exceptional physiotherapist who has won numerous awards for his research into burns therapy.

CHAPTER 22

Family support

*'Many people will walk in and out of your life,
but only true friends will leave footprints in your heart.'*

- Eleanor Roosevelt -

When you are laid up for an extended period, you learn who your true friends are. These are the people who stick by you through thick and thin and provide you with unconditional love whatever the situation. My hospital life was broken up by visits from my immediate family – my mother and brother – but also my cousins Ante, Maria (dec.) and Yerko Radic came to the hospital almost every day to see me. Ante, in particular, was a tower of strength and guidance during this period. I am forever grateful for the unconditional love and support they offered during this tumultuous period.

On many occasions my mother would bring chicken soup with her when she visited, as she believed it had special healing powers that could heal the most stubborn of wounds. My brother jokingly called it 'Croatian antibiotics', but I always scoffed the soup down as it was a welcome change from the hospital menu. The power of the chicken soup also won over nurse Georgie, who would pay me a visit whenever

she smelled the soup from her desk. Georgie had a smile that could brighten up the darkest of days, so it was always a double delight for me.

During my hospital stay I had many visitors, including my Godparents, Ante and Katija Jakovcevic, along with friends and work colleagues. I also received hundreds of cards and messages of support, mostly from people I didn't even know. It seemed as though the tragedy had struck a chord with many people, and when the Zanetic family, who were family friends, organised a book of messages for me, I was touched by the words of encouragement and empathy shown. However, of all the messages I received, the one that stood out the most was a letter of support from legendary Manchester United coach, Sir Alex Ferguson. In it, he wrote that I should listen to my doctors and that he and the players were thinking of me. Even though I am a Liverpool fan, I was buoyed by the letter of support.

On 1 March 2005, Perth had a Royal visitor – His Royal Highness Prince Charles. A group of survivors were invited to meet with him at

RPH. As I had never met anyone regal in my life, I took up the offer. Initially I was a bit nervous, not knowing what to say, but he turned out to be a very calm and easy person to talk to, and he genuinely seemed interested in our stories of survival. When Prof. Wood stepped in and told him I was the 'star of the show', I was lost for words.

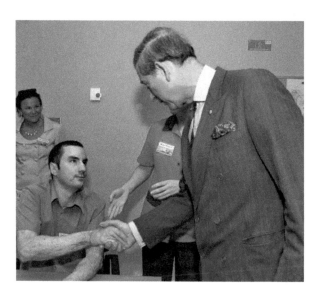

CHAPTER 23

Outpatient

'Triumphant Bali survivor limps home for a coldie'

- The Age -[23]

The 6th of January 2003 was a memorable day, as the doctors had decided I was mobile enough to head home. It was time for me to pack up my few belongings and end my tenure as an inpatient. After saying my goodbyes and thank-yous to the nursing staff, I headed down the hallway, aided by a walking stick and accompanied by my brother and mother. We took the lift to the ground level, and after walking up a small hallway and then turning left into the main passage, I was greeted by a group of fellow survivors who had organised a guard of honour to commemorate the last Bali patient to leave hospital in Western Australia. The local TV reporters went into a frenzy as they snapped pictures of me walking out of hospital after two months and 21 days as an inpatient. I held a short press conference with them in the hospital foyer, and they asked me a series of questions about my

---

[23]'Triumphant Bali survivor limps home for a coldie', *The Age*, 7 January 2003, *https://www.theage.com.au/national/triumphant-bali-survivor-limps-home-for-a-coldie-20030107-gdv166. html*, accessed 27 June, 2018.

hospital stay and survival; however, when one of them asked me what I was most looking forward to when I got home, I quipped 'a nice cold beer' and so *The Age* headline for the next day read, 'Triumphant Bali survivor limps home for a coldie'.[24]

Being at home and in the comfort of my own surroundings was a great step forward for my rehabilitation, but even though I was out of hospital, rehab was far from over. I was now considered an outpatient and had to go to hospital daily for dressing changes, physio and occupational therapy. Every day I would get a taxi to RPH, and the first stop at 9am would be the outpatient clinic for a dressing change. The clinic was usually busy so the wait to see the doctor and get my dressings changed could take up to four hours. Some of my remaining wounds were very stubborn and took a long time to heal. The wound on my left elbow took almost seven months to heal.

After a quick bite to eat, I would then head down to the physiotherapy building for one hour of hand physio followed by one hour of occupational therapy. Once this was completed, it would be off to the gym for one hour of exercise. By 3pm I would be well and truly exhausted and ready to head home. This became my routine for the next 10 months, as I continued daily rehabilitation to regain movement in all parts of my body. The only time this routine was interrupted was when I needed more surgery.

Despite the physios' best efforts, there were still some problem areas around my body, which needed surgical intervention. In 2003 I had four operations, with the most memorable being on 13 October. My left hand had borne the brunt of my burn injury, and after months of physio the fingers still would not bend at the knuckle joint, and my hand had an uncontrollable tremble, making it difficult to hold items such as a knife and fork. To compensate for this, I would strap

---

[24]Ibid.

a fork to my wrist joint and use my wrist movements rather than my fingers. To rectify this issue, Prof. Wood's expertise was once again called upon. The surgery involved placing a full thickness graft, taken from my waist, behind my left knuckles and around the inside of my left thumb. At the same time, they performed a Z-plasty (scar revision procedure) along my left rib cage and released the skin under my armpits as well. Prof. Wood then injected Botox into the left hand, which had the effect of detaching the nerves where they joined the muscle. The idea being that once the nerves grew back, they would reattach themselves to a different part of the muscle and the trembling would stop. On the day following the surgery, Prof. Wood and her entourage, which included Dr Mark Duncan-Smith, came in to see me, and knowing it was my 27th birthday, they broke out into song. I was lost for words as they belted out a rip-roaring 'Happy Birthday'.

Fellow plastic surgeon Dr Anna Goodwin-Walters later told me the operation had gone well but it was a real mission to get my hand to bend to place the graft. She said Prof. Wood used all her strength to bend the hand and after much trying it finally gave way. In many ways this sums up Prof. Fiona Wood: always putting in maximum effort to get the best result for her patients.

CHAPTER 24

The psychological impact

*'Our mind is a garden, our thoughts are the seeds,
you can grow flowers, or you can grow weeds.'*

- Ritu Ghatourey -

According to the World Health Organization, mental health is 'A state of wellbeing in which every individual realises his or her own potential, can cope with the normal stresses of life, can work productively and fruitfully, and is able to make a contribution to his or her community.'[25]

In all, it took 28 operations (12 x laser and 16 x surgical) over 19 years to repair the damage to my body caused by the Sari Club bomb, but the psychological impact will last a lifetime. It didn't affect me initially, whilst I was preoccupied with recovering from my physical injuries; it was some years later when I developed Post-Traumatic Stress Disorder (PTSD).

---

[25]World Health Organization (2022). 'Mental health: strengthening our response', 17 June 2022. *https://www.who.int/news-room/fact-sheets/detail/mental-health-strengthening-our-response*, accessed 5 January 2021.

PTSD is a delayed reaction to trauma that has occurred sometime in your life. It is common in soldiers who have returned from war zones such as Vietnam and Afghanistan. The hippocampus is the part of the brain responsible for storing long-term memory; however, it does not 'file away' traumatic events. Instead, it stores them in the subconscious mind and keeps replaying them over and over on a continuous loop. Events that may have occurred as long as 40 years ago can still be at the forefront of a person's mind, especially if the memory is traumatic. This is why many returned veterans suffer from PTSD-related symptoms years after their service. In hindsight, I would say the psychological impact is worse than the physical injury, simply because it gnaws at you constantly like a dog with a bone. People deal with it in different ways; some turn to drugs and alcohol, others to medication – some don't deal with it at all.

On my last trip to Bali in 2018, I met a Balinese survivor who told me she had attempted suicide on seven occasions, which I think is rather sad. The Balinese victims never received the same support as we did in Australia; in fact, the Indonesian Government only offered them some compensation in 2019.

Personally, I had only thought about suicide once. I was on a cruise ship in the middle of the Pacific, I should have been having the time of my life, but I was at the lowest point of my life. The day was idyllic, seas were calm, the sun was shining, and the thought had crossed my mind...why don't I jump off this ship into the wild blue yonder, never to be seen again? As I looked down at the swirling water behind the propellers - I talked myself out of it. I had come too far in my rehabilitation to call it quits now and besides, the thought of being chewed up by the giant propellers wasn't very appealing.

The hallmarks of my PTSD were intrusive thoughts, which created anxiety resulting in muscle tension and high blood pressure (hypertension). The anxiety caused me to feel fear when I was actually safe, which in turn would trigger the fight/flight/freeze response. Quite often, thoughts of hostile situations would play out in my head to the point where I would suddenly clench my fists and grit my teeth, in preparation for a battle that would never eventuate. The battle was being played out in my head and, like most things medical, it had a scientific explanation.

'A traumatic event is any experience in which a person is exposed to, or witnesses, a threatening or harmful event, and experiences strong negative emotions and helplessness...the emotions and bodily reactions at the time of the traumatic event are associated with chemicals in the nervous system, including adrenaline, and these cause the brain to store or encode the traumatic experience in a manner different from an everyday event which doesn't carry a strong emotional charge.'[26]

'The part of the brain responsible for controlling emotional responses is called the amygdala and is an almond shaped structure situated in the mid-brain, forming part of the limbic system. This structure plays a role in fear and the fight or flight response'.[27] 'The amygdala can be stimulated when faced with a perceived threat. If in a threatening situation, the amygdala will send information to other parts of the brain to prepare the body to either face the situation, or to get away from it. This fight-or-flight response is triggered by emotions of fear, anxiety, aggression, and anger. It is beneficial that the amygdala is working correctly in order to act appropriately in threatening or stressful situations. However, sometimes the amygdala can act too strongly, leading to amygdala hijacking'.[28]

---

[26]Heath, Dr J. (n.d.). 'Trauma', *https://www.janheath.com.au/clinical-services/trauma/*, accessed 16 September 2021.
[27]Guy-Evans, O. (2021). 'Amygdala Hijack and the Fight or Flight Response', *Simply Psychology*, 5 November 2021, *www.simplypsychology.org/what-happens-during-an-amygdala-hijack.html*, accessed 27 June 2022.
[28]Guy-Evans, O. (2021). 'Amygdala function and location', *Simply Psychology*, 9 May 2021, *www.simplypsychology.org/amygdala.html*, accessed 27 June 2022.

For people living with PTSD the amygdala can be activated by 'triggers', which is anything that is connected to the initial trauma. These triggers include things such as sounds, people arguing, news reports and even subsequent negative events. When the amygdala is activated, it can affect the way people think, how they feel and how they behave. 'The symptoms of amygdala hijack are because of the body's chemical response to stress. The hormone released by the adrenal glands, cortisol, and epinephrine, prepare the body to fight-or-flight and have an effect on the body:

- Rapid heart rate
- Clammy skin
- Dilated pupils to improve vision for faster responses
- Sweating
- Goosebumps on the skin
- Increased blood sugar – for immediate energy
- Contracted blood vessels allow the body to redirect blood to major muscle groups
- Airways expand to allow in and use more oxygen.

The result of amygdala hijack can cause behaviours which are considered irrational for the situation such as shouting, verbal abuse, or crying'.[29]

Learning how to manage and reduce the symptoms of PTSD is a very slow process and takes time to do. This is because tackling PTSD means gently and consistently retraining our brains and bodies not to trigger PTSD symptoms when we are no longer in danger. There are various distraction techniques available to help reduce the adverse effects of the amygdala. Using controlled breathing exercises, meditation and exercising regularly are all recognised ways of restoring a sense of calm and physical relaxation. The focus is on the interactions between the mind, body, and behaviour.

---

[29]Guy-Evans, O. (2021). 'Amygdala Hijack and the Fight or Flight Response', op cit.

'Breathing can be a powerful tool during a heightened situation as it can trigger the parasympathetic nervous system to bring about a restful bodily response. Taking control of breathing in stressful situations can allow thoughtful decisions which are not driven be emotions'.[30] The extra oxygen in the lungs is carried to the brain and enables the brain to relax more. The trick is to do this regularly when you feel anxiety or nervous tension coming on.

Meditation is another good way of slowing down the over-arousal symptoms associated with PTSD. Although, you don't have to sit under a pyramid to do this like the character Shirley Gilroy (Lorrae Desmond (dec.) in *A Country Practice*. Meditation can take many forms, and one of my favourites is fishing. Being out on the boat and wetting a line, I am in touch with nature and breathing fresh air. Even if I don't catch anything, I know I am benefiting from it.

Exercise is also another great way of reducing anxiety and improving your mental health. 'Evidence suggests that by really focusing on your body and how it feels as you exercise, you can actually help your nervous system become "unstuck" and begin to move out of the immobilization stress response that characterizes PTSD or trauma. Exercises that involve cross movement and that engage both arms and legs—such as walking (especially in sand), running, swimming, weight training, or dancing—are some of your best choices'.[31]

In the years following my PTSD diagnosis I took on many activities, including ball room dancing, pilates, martial arts and meditation to help manage the symptoms. When trying to manage PTSD symptoms I have found that persistence and consistency is the key to success. You can't expect to get results overnight, but the more you engage with the strategies the better the results.

---

[30]Ibid.

[31]Robinson, L., Segal, J. & Smith, M. (2021). 'Help Guide - The Mental Health Benefits of Exercise', HelpGuide, August 2021, *https://www.helpguide.org/articles/healthy-living/the-mental-health-benefits-of-exercise.htm?platform=hootsuite&pdf=13390*, accessed 25 June 2022.

CHAPTER 25

Psychological treatment

*'Acknowledging the good that you already have in your life
is the foundation for all abundance.'*

- Eckhart Tolle -[32]

Our brain is the root of our body; it controls everything from movement, to thoughts and feelings. By having a healthy mind, we can deal with the most difficult of situations and prevail through hard times. But just how do you rebuild a healthy mind when it has been compromised by a traumatic event? The good news is the brain is not hardwired, and it can be modified to adapt to a change in circumstances. In the world of medical science this is known as neuroplasticity.

In his studies of animal behaviour, anthropologist Charles Darwin made two important discoveries. The first was 'survival of the fittest', and the second was that animals that could adapt to a change in their surroundings are the ones that are most likely to survive. The book

[32]Tolle, E. (2005). *A New Earth: Awakening to Your Life's Purpose,*
Viking Press (New York City, New York, USA).

Who Moved My Cheese? by Spencer Johnson, highlights this fact.[33] It is a story about two mice who would use the same pathway in a maze to get to a supply of cheese; however, one day the path was blocked and the mice had to find another way to get to the cheese. One of the mice went about exploring and found another path to the cheese, whilst the other mouse continued to use the same path each day only to find it was blocked. Suffice it to say, we all know which mouse survived.

Throughout my journey of recovery I have tried a variety of ways to heal my PTSD symptoms, with varied success. Initially, my psychological treatment consisted of Cognitive Behavioural Therapy (CBT), which focuses on reducing the symptoms of the anxiety attack. This includes focusing on your breathing or on the natural environment, to draw your attention away from those negative thoughts and focus it on the 'here and now'. CBT was useful in reducing the severity of my anxiety attacks, but it didn't deal with the root cause of the trauma.

Another therapy I tried was The Richards Trauma Process (TRTP), which at $450.00 a session wasn't cheap. It involved mild hypnosis where the therapist would try to trick my brain into thinking the trauma was over, and that it was now time to move on. The idea was to introduce new brain patterns, so that the old brain patterns causing the trauma were no longer stimulated. This treatment relies on listening to the therapist intently, but with my concentration issues I couldn't focus well on her commentary. Quite often I would experience disassociation where my mind would wander off in other directions, so the treatment was not successful for me.

Another technique I tried was called Eye Movement Desensitisation and Reprocessing (EMDR), which like the TRTP approach attempts to manipulate brain patterns. The idea is to reduce the stimulation of

---

[33]Johnson, S. (1998). *Who Moved My Cheese? An Amazing Way to Deal with Change in Your Work and in Your Life*, Putnam Adult (New York City, New York, USA).

brain patterns that are causing the anxiety issues and create new brain patterns that are healthier and more positive. During my EMDR treatment, the therapist asked me to recall my thoughts, emotions and the bodily sensations related to the trauma. I was then asked to follow the moving fingers of the therapist for 30 seconds. My eyes would move rapidly during this time, producing a distinctive pattern of electrical activity in the brain, which resulted in a change to the trauma memory. How the brain causes the memory to change has not yet been discovered, but the regions of the brain involved with sensory storage, emotional activation and reasoning, all become more active with changed patterns of nerve cell firing.[34]

I found EMDR interesting, but it wasn't effective enough in dealing with the negative thoughts that kept appearing from my subconscious mind. You may have heard the term 'think positive' being bandied around by motivational coaches, and although positive thoughts can strengthen good brain patterns, they cannot stop the subconscious mind from bringing up negative thoughts. This is because the traumatic experiences carry more emotion than positive thoughts and although the conscious mind realises that the trauma is over, the subconscious mind keeps bringing up the thoughts at random.

I also tried a technique called Emotional Freedom Technique (EFT), which involves tapping on the meridian points on your body to apply pressure. 'Based on Chinese medicine, meridian points are thought of as areas of the body energy flows through. These pathways help balance energy flow to maintain your health. Any imbalance can influence disease or sickness'.[35] Proponents say the tapping helps you

---

[34]Taylor, G. (2003). 'Resolving Trauma with EMDR', Pathways of Mind website, *https://pathwaysofmind.com/healing-from-trauma/emdr/graham-taylor-resolving-trauma-with-emdr/*, accessed 4 October 2021.
[35]Healthline (2017). 'EFT Tapping', *https://www.healthline.com/health/eft-tapping*, accessed 11 December 2021.

access your body's energy and send signals to the part of the brain that controls stress. They claim that stimulating the meridian points through EFT tapping can reduce the stress or negative emotion you feel from your issue, ultimately restoring balance to your disrupted energy.

The EFT tapping sequence is the methodical tapping on the ends of nine meridian points. There are 12 major meridians that mirror each side of the body and correspond to an internal organ. However, EFT mainly focuses on these nine:

1. Karate chop (KC): small intestine meridian
2. Top of head (TH): governing vessel
3. Eyebrow (EB): bladder meridian
4. Side of the eye (SE): gallbladder meridian
5. Under the eye (UE): stomach meridian
6. Under the nose (UN): governing vessel
7. Chin (Ch): central vessel
8. Beginning of the collarbone (CB): kidney meridian
9. Under the arm (UA): spleen meridian.

Whilst doing the tapping you recite a script that explains what you are trying to address. The script focuses on two main goals:

1. Acknowledging the issues
2. Accepting yourself despite the problem.

Although, the tapping looks rather 'silly', I found it quite beneficial in refocusing my mind and thus reducing the severity of the intrusive thoughts I was having; however, it didn't stop the thoughts from reappearing.

Hence, after trying all these different techniques with varied amounts of success, I came to the conclusion that I would be stuck with these intrusive thoughts for the rest of my life and there was nothing I could do to fix it.

I eventually turned to a relatively new form of treatment called Acceptance and Commitment Therapy (ACT). The goal of ACT is to create a rich and meaningful life, whilst accepting the pain that invariably goes with it. It is similar to CBT in that it uses mindfulness as a tool. However, it does not try to reduce the symptoms, it simply acknowledges them.

ACT uses six core principles to help clients develop psychological flexibility:

1. Defusion
2. Acceptance
3. Contact with the present moment
4. Observing Self
5. Values
6. Committed Action.[36]

The principle of mindfulness teaches people to live in the moment and engage fully with what you are doing, rather than getting lost in your thoughts. It allows your feelings to be as they are, letting them come and go rather than trying to control them.

ACT taught me that anxiety is just a normal emotional response, just like thoughts of happiness, sadness and anger. 'Some people try to reduce the effects of anxiety by using emotional control strategies, such as drinking alcohol or turning to drugs; however, these strategies can be self-destructive in the long term'.

It is believed there are at least 6000 thoughts that pass through the human brain every day.[37] Ninety per cent of these thoughts are the same today as they were yesterday, and 80 per cent of them are negative.

---

[36]Harris, R. (2011). 'Embracing Your Demons: An Overview of Acceptance and Commitment Therapy', Psychotherapy.net, *https://www.psychotherapy.net/article/Acceptance-and-Commitment-Therapy-ACT*, accessed 27 June 2021.
[37]Pittman, S. (2020). 'New study suggests people have more than 6000 thoughts per day', 16 July 2020, The Mighty, *https://themighty.com/2020/07/study-how-many-thoughts-per-day/*, accessed 26 June 2020.

'In a state of cognitive fusion we are caught up in or preoccupied with thoughts, which can then have enormous influence over our behaviour. Cognitive defusion enables us to step back psychologically and observe thoughts without being caught up in them'.[38] There are many defusion techniques available, for example, whenever a negative thought pops into your head you say, 'Thank you, Mind' and then carry on with whatever you were doing. There is no need to dwell on the thought or analyse it, just accept it and move on. One of the simplest analogies of this process is likening your brain to a freeway system, where every day there are thousands of cars passing through. The cars represent all your thoughts; however, occasionally, a fire truck may come past with sirens blaring. The fire truck represents a negative thought, which may cause you distress. By using ACT principles, you simply acknowledge the fire truck and allow it to pass, you don't try to stop it.

Identifying your values is also an important part of the ACT process. Values are those things we believe in and determine how we want to behave as a human being. Your values can be difficult to identify; they may require some soul searching, but once you define them, they can help your life become more meaningful. Put simply, values reflect what we want to do and how we want to do it. Some of my personal values included courage, contribution, respect, humility, mindfulness and gratitude.

One of the best things I ever did was to talk openly about my thoughts with people whom I could trust. I have visited many psychologists over the past ten years, all of whom provided guidance on how to approach the issues I was experiencing. The best advice I can give is to 'shop around' and try different therapies until you find something that works for you.

---

[38]Harris, Dr R. (2009). 'Mindfulness without meditation', *HCPJ*, *https://www.actmindfully.com.au/upimages/Mindfulness_without_meditation_--_Russ_Harris_--_HCPJ_Oct_09.pdf*, accessed 20 May 2022.

In my career as an occupational health and safety professional, I have talked to people about my experiences with anxiety and helped my current employer develop a mental health strategy.

'Statistics show that on average, one in four people – one in three women and one in five men – will experience an anxiety condition at some stage in their life'[39], but this is only based on the cases that are reported. The true figure is much higher because many people don't talk about their mental health struggles. The fact is, we are all made of flesh and blood, and things that happen to us can overwhelm us, so it is best to talk about your issues and seek professional help if you are feeling overburdened with life.

If these two chapters have stirred up personal issues or caused you distress, help is available.

In Australia call:
Lifeline - 13 11 14
Beyond Blue - 1300 224 636

[39]Reavley, N., Morgan, A., Jorm, A., Wright, J., Bassilios, B., Hopwood, M., Allen, N. & Purcell, R. (2010). *Beyond Blue - A guide that works for anxiety, https://learn.beyondblue-elearning.org.au/workplace/resources/pdf/topic5/GuideToWhatWorksForAnxiety.pdf,* accessed 5 February 2021.

CHAPTER 26

Post-traumatic growth

*'I am not fully healed, I am not fully wise, I am still on my way.
What matters is that I am moving forward.'*

- Yung Pueblo -[40]

When a major bushfire sweeps through a forest it destroys everything in its path, leaving behind a blackened landscape. However, with a bit of sunshine and a steady supply of water reaching the roots of the tree, it's not long before the forest starts to regrow. Similarly, people who have suffered a burn injury can recover as well. One thing that being sick for an extended period has taught me is that your health and wellbeing are your most important assets in life.

To help me to recover from PTSD, I had to understand what my personal values were, and how I could use those in a form of committed action to adapt to the change in my circumstances. By employing a strategy of psychological adaptation, I was able to change my mindset from an inward perspective to a more outward view, away

---

[40]Pueblo, Y. (n.d.), located at D. Sy on Pinterest,
https://www.pinterest.com.au/pin/358317714104584506/, accessed 5 May 2022.

from being consumed by my own thoughts. In the years after my traumatic injury, I took on many different activities including public speaking, volunteering, further education and helping with medical research, to create the type of positive mindset that spurs new growth. The main benefit I got from these activities was post-traumatic growth, which helped to reduce those negative and hostile thoughts that were overwhelming my mindset.

Public speaking is a good way to tell your story because it can help you make sense of the whole experience. In the first few years after my injury, I think I told my story a hundred times over because almost everyone was interested in what happened. This can become quite annoying, but at the same time I can understand why people are interested.

However, talking was never one of my strong points, in fact, my year one report card said that I was a 'quiet but conscientious student'. To help rectify my speaking phobia, I joined the Victoria Quay branch of Toastmasters International. Toastmasters is an organisation that helps people overcome their speaking anxiety. The great thing about Toastmasters is that you realise you are not alone with your phobia; in fact, studies show that public speaking is the biggest phobia for most people.[41] My group met every Wednesday night, and participants worked through a competent communication manual that guided us through the various forms of speaking. Not only did we improve our speaking skills, but we also got to network with other people from all walks of life. I later put my public speaking skills to the test when I attended a seminar on counter-terrorism in Bali. I gave a speech outlining my experience in the bombings and why it was important for countries to work together to defeat the scourge of terrorism.

---

[41]National Social Anxiety Center (n.d.). 'Public Speaking Anxiety', *https://nationalsocialanxietycenter.com/social-anxiety/public-speaking-anxiety/*, accessed 30 June 2022.

I have also spent time talking to other burn survivors about their injuries and how they can aid their recovery. I found that kids in particular don't really understand the nature of a burn injury, and how wearing face masks and burn suits can help with their recovery. In 2019, I met a young boy named Koby, who had suffered burns to his face, upper body and hands, when a tablecloth caught fire. Koby wouldn't wear his face mask because it was uncomfortable and quite frankly embarrassing when he was around other kids. After having a good chat with him and showing him some of my scars, Koby felt a lot better about his injuries and regained confidence that he would recover. I also made a pact with Koby that if he wore his mask, I would wear mine and lo and behold, the next day he sent me a photo of him with his face mask on.

Volunteering is also a great way of changing your perspective to more of an outward view, as there is no greater feeling than to be helping someone else. In 2016, I joined an organisation called Fishability, which helps disabled people learn the art of fishing. Helping these people, some with lifelong conditions such as cerebral palsy, muscular dystrophy and quadriplegia, put things into perspective for me. It showed me that there are people out there who are doing it tougher than most, but who still have the courage and strength to give life their best shot.

Community Involvement is all about making a positive contribution to the community you live in. It is an important part of life. In 2017, I joined the local crime prevention group and quickly earned respect amongst the existing members by developing a Facebook page, which at the time of writing has 3859 followers. The page provides crime prevention information to the general public.

Later that year, I reformed the Spearwood Progress Association, a local community group representing the residents of Spearwood in matters with the Cockburn Council. I was voted president, unanimously, four years running, and I have guided the association in achieving some major improvements for the suburb. Volunteering opened new doors for me, and I was able to meet some inspiring people who became great friends.

'Studies show that through improved social connections and a sense of purpose, volunteering provides a feeling of belonging and can stimulate both mental and physical wellbeing. Social connections made through volunteer positions are often lifelong and additional skills picked up through volunteer roles can help with employment and career progression'.[42] In early 2020, I secured a job in local government, from a field of over one hundred applicants, partly because I volunteered in the community.

Further study after trauma can also be a good way to refocus the mind, gain more knowledge and move forward in life. After my injury, I didn't feel like going back to my old job because the stress and long hours involved took time away from more meaningful things. So, I decided to take on further studies to pursue a more purposeful career. Over the years I've completed postgraduate and diploma courses in occupational health and safety, leadership, management and training that have set me up for a successful career.

By using my personal values in the form of committed action I was able to experience post-traumatic growth which helped with my recovery. Your personal values, are like the roots of a tree, they are at the core of who you are and what you do. As long as you stay true to yourself and committed to your values you can use them to change your life for the better.

---

[42] Edgar, S., (2021). 'The benefits of volunteering for your mental health', 6 July 2021, Lifeline WA, *https://wa.lifeline.org.au/resources/helpful-articles/the-benefits-of-volunteering-for-your-mental-health/*, accessed 26 June 2022.

Post-traumatic research

To see how patients change after their injury and whether they experience positive psychological change or growth a study was carried out by Burn researcher Lisa Martin. This type of change is called post-traumatic growth (PTG) and happens because of a struggle with a traumatic event.

To help understand the psychological impact of a burn injury, I volunteered for the study, which explored what positive changes are experienced by burn injury survivors and how these changes occur. This information will help to encourage growth for burn patients in the future. The study involved filling out questionnaires based on quality of life, the Depression Anxiety Stress Scale (DASS), the Post-Traumatic Growth Inventory (PTGI), and the Burn-Specific Health-Scale Brief (BSHS-B). The result was a publication entitled Life after Burn, produced from the input of all participants and readily available to all new burn patients to assist them with their recovery.

CHAPTER 27

Managing public perceptions

'I am not what happened to me, I am what I choose to become.'

- Carl Gustav Jung -

Being a burn survivor, particularly from a terror attack, tends to attract a lot of attention, especially from the media. I must admit when I came out of hospital on 6 January 2003 and entered the main hall of RPH, I was not expecting a throng of media to be waiting for me with a stack of cameras pointed at my face. This was a level of scrutiny I had never experienced before in my life and it was quite daunting.

The media see burn survival stories as publicity because they always draw attention, which means more advertising space can be sold in newspapers and on TV. Being able to handle the sudden attention is not always easy, and you have to be careful with the words you choose because people will always remember the 'slip-ups' more than the actual story. And it's not just the media that you need to deal with, but also members of the public. People often ask what happened to me. Once, after having a Z-plasty (scar revision procedure) on the left side of my face, which had left a fairly large Z-shaped incision on my left neck and face, I was walking through a park when a young kid on a bike, standing about 30 metres away, shouted out to me.

'What happened to the side of your face?'

So, you find yourself telling your story over and over again, which can become quite annoying, but for the public it is intriguing. Why do people ask? Well, humans are inquisitive by nature and will always ask questions. Some may even think about how they would survive if they were ever caught up in a terror attack. Quite often you may be asked the question, do you see yourself as a victim or a survivor? This is an interesting question that has a psychological aspect to it. If you feel you are a *victim*, you may always feel sorry for yourself and find it difficult to move on, but if you see yourself as a *survivor*, you can focus on the positive aspects of your ordeal, which can set you up for a better recovery. I see myself as both a victim *and* a survivor. When the bomb went off and I was badly injured, I became a victim of the attack, but as I went through my rehabilitation, I underwent a transformation and became a survivor.

One of the feelings that a survivor can experience is a psychological reaction known as survivor's guilt. This is where the victim questions why they survived when so many others didn't. In the case of the Bali bombings, there were more than 350 survivors of the attacks. How many of these people experienced survivor's guilt is not known, but what is known is that survivor's guilt can be debilitating, and some people feel that they have to justify their existence by doing things such as climbing mountains, running marathons, or supporting charities. In reality, people survive near-death experiences every day for a multitude of reasons. In my opinion, you never have to do anything to justify your existence on this earth. You have as much right to be on this planet as anyone else, and the fact that you survived and others died, comes down to pure luck.

I have always found that being open and honest about my story is the best policy. There is no point sugar-coating it or trying to hide it, just tell it as it is. The majority of people will be sympathetic and if they are not, well, who cares? what matters is how you feel. I believe that telling your story either verbally or in print can be cathartic and will help with your psychological recovery.

CHAPTER 28

Pushing the boundaries

'A ship in harbour is safe, but that is not what ships are built for.'
- John A. Shedd -

In life, the only boundaries we have are those that we place in front of ourselves. If you want to get ahead in life, whether it be in your chosen career or with personal development, you have to learn to push the boundaries. However, to push boundaries you must first identify and confront them. Whether it be the fear of learning to walk again, a fear of public speaking or the fear of talking about your anxiety issues, to overcome these fears you must be prepared to face up to them; only then can you conquer them.

When Prof. Wood, and scientist Marie Stoner invented spray-on-skin, they pushed the boundaries of medical science through a new frontier and invented something no-one else had ever thought of. This shows there are always scientific discoveries to be made – and it's only through research we can make big strides in medicine.

One of the stumbling blocks to research is often money, or lack thereof. In 2021, to raise funds for the Fiona Wood Foundation, I was invited to participate in the Central Park Plunge: a controlled descent down the tallest building in Perth. The task involved abseiling, commando style, 220 metres down the side of Central Park Tower. Now, I'd like to point out that I'm certainly no commando; I usually get jittery standing on a ladder, but I was prepared to push the boundaries and give it a go.

On the day of the abseil, I arrived at the tower about half an hour early, just to get a feel for it, and saw other participants coming down the building. All of a sudden I was starting to have second thoughts. But fear not, at 2:30 pm, the team of four I was grouped with took the lift to the fifty-first floor and had an induction followed by fit-out. After that it was a short practice run on firm ground, just to make sure we knew what to do and, more importantly, what not to do.

The abseil company had setup a scaffold on the edge of the building, which meant as I began, my feet didn't touch the side of the building, which for some reason made me feel safer, but nevertheless still quite daunted. The hardest part was letting myself go backwards towards the ground from 220 metres up – it isn't natural, but it's exhilarating at the same time. About five metres down, the abseil team told us to let go of our rope and place our arms out wide for the 'Money Shot'. I completed the plunge successfully and I must admit, coming down the last 20 metres I was a bit teary-eyed. The fact that 19 years

earlier I had been unable to change channels on the TV remote and now I was able to abseil down the tallest building in Perth. This is testament to the many doctors, nurses and allied health professionals who have treated me over the years.

CHAPTER 29

Defiance

*'In War: Resolution; In Defeat: Defiance; In Victory: Magnanimity;
In Peace: Goodwill.'*

- Sir Winston Churchill -

On graduating from high school in 1993, my Year 12 History teacher, Mr Whittamseth, awarded me the Winston Churchill Medal for displaying great courage and conviction in my studies of world history. At the time I had no idea I would need to draw upon that courage later in life.

In the aftermath of the Bali bombings, the Balinese tourism industry was decimated, and locals struggled to survive with less tourism dollars. Tourism is something that brings people together and by learning more about other cultures it makes us less likely to engage in acts of racism and hatred. Hence, the best thing to do is to counter this fear by going about your daily lives as normal and if possible, to travel widely throughout the world.

I have been lucky enough to travel throughout the world and will always remember my overseas adventures as being a great learning experience. In 2007, I flew to Europe for a six-week holiday, to see my extended family in Croatia and visit some of the Eastern Bloc countries. The fourteen-day tour of these countries took in Germany, Austria, Czech Republic, Hungary and Poland. Whilst in Poland, I visited the Auschwitz concentration camp where Nazis murdered millions of people. This was an experience I will never forget. The camp was the most eerie and daunting place I had ever been to in my life, and I could sense the terrible things that occurred there during the Second World War.

In 2011, I travelled to the United States and spent four weeks on the West Coast. I visited San Diego, the Grand Canyon, Las Vegas, Yosemite National Park, San Francisco and Los Angeles, and then headed east to New York and Washington D.C. Whilst in New York, the tour guide took us to the ground zero site where the World Trade Centre towers once stood. They were demolished by terrorists on 11 September 2001, killing 2893 civilians in the process. The guide described how events unfolded on that day, and then took us to a small church nearby, which had survived the destruction because it was protected by a large tree. Some describe this as a miracle because everything else around the site was destroyed, apart from that small church.

I took a helicopter tour of New York and whilst in the air, I began to imagine what it would have been like for those people on board the planes that crashed into the towers on that fateful day. The 9/11 attacks were the start of an international terror campaign launched by Al-Qaeda and its affiliates worldwide. I was glad I could visit the site and pay my respects to those who had been the first victims in this cowardly, barbaric and senseless act of violence against innocent people who were simply going about their daily lives.

Although many of the survivors of the Bali bombings have been back to Bali on numerous occasions since the attack, I had never really felt the urge to go back until the Australian Government invited all survivors and their families to return for the tenth anniversary on 12 October 2012. Initially, I was in two minds about heading back to the island that had almost claimed my life, as thoughts of another possible attack played out in my mind. But after much deliberation, I decided I would go back and revisit the site. I wanted to retrace my steps and piece together some of the gaps I still had of that fateful night. To offer support and make things easier for me, Steve Bakovic, Deanna Thompson and my brother accompanied me to attend the event as well. Once we'd arrived in Bali, my nerves soon settled as we bunkered down at the five-Star Park Royal Beach Hotel in Seminyak.

On the day of the anniversary, we were picked up by buses at a predetermined location. Security for the event was unprecedented, with each bus having an armed police officer on board and a police escort to the ceremony, which was held in an old quarry nestled on a hilltop in Jimbaran Bay. The ceremony was well organised and included speeches by many dignitaries including the then Australian Prime Minister Julia Gillard; Indonesia's foreign minister Marty Negawarta; and former Australian Prime Minister John Howard. After the event we headed back to Kuta to the memorial site to place some flowers. The memorial was impressive and built directly across the road from the former Sari Club and Paddy's Bar – the names of all the victims were inscribed and it was covered with hundreds of flowers from people paying their respects.

After leaving the memorial, I retraced my steps on that night. With Steve and Deanna in tow, we went down to the Bali cottages car park, where Steve had found me. We strolled past our hotel, Troppo Zone, and talked about that eventful night and how we had all managed to survive. The trip back to Bali was a soul-cleansing experience that closed a lot of the gaps, and it certainly helped with my recovery.

CHAPTER 30

Ten tips for surviving burns trauma

*'God, grant me the serenity to accept the things I cannot change,
courage to change the things I can,
and wisdom to know the difference.'*

- Serenity Prayer by Reinhold Niebuhr -

Life is full of experiences, good and bad. Sometimes it can throw curve balls at you when you least expect it. These curve balls may include illness, injury, divorce, redundancy, or the death of a loved one. These experiences are quite common, but the way you deal with them defines your strength of character.

Recovering from a major burn injury is no easy feat, and you need good medical care along with supportive family and friends. But there is also a lot the patient can do to help their recovery, and to prosper after such a major trauma. Here are my top ten tips:

1) **Accept what has happened to you.** This can take some time but the sooner you do it, the better. Once you have accepted what has happened, you can then change your mindset to that of recovery. You can't change what has happened, but you can define how you will deal with it, which then affects how well you recover.

2) **Listen to the medical staff.** This is crucial to achieve the best result for your injury. These people have spent many years studying medicine and have seen injuries far worse than yours, so do as they tell you and if you're not sure of anything, ask questions.

3) **Believe in yourself.** Self-belief is important; you don't realise how strong you are until you are challenged. Self-doubt can creep into your mind during the recovery phase but remember these are just thoughts, not reality.

4) **Show self-compassion.** This is just as important as self-belief. Don't beat yourself up over the injury. Accidents happen, it might have been a silly little mistake that caused it, but there is no point chastising yourself over it. Your focus should be on recovery, not playing the blame game on yourself.

5) **Have the right attitude.** This is very important as there is only so much the doctors and nurses can do for you. Examples of having the right attitude include doing 'bed exercises' when the physios aren't around and wearing the pressure suit 24 hours a day for as long as it's needed. Even though this is inconvenient and uncomfortable, it is necessary to reduce the scarring.

6) **Be patient, it's a virtue.** It can take some time to get the joints to bend again after a severe burn injury, but more often than not they eventually give way.

7) **Persevere.** You must be prepared to dig in for the long haul and for setbacks along the way. I had many stubborn wounds, some that took up to seven months to fully heal, but in the end they all came good.

8) **Show gratitude.** Quite often we don't realise the effect a burn injury has on those around us, or the amount of time and effort that people have put in to help us out. So, always show gratitude to those who help you, especially your doctors and family.

9) **Don't compare yourself to others.** A burn injury is not a sprint to the finish line; rather, it's a marathon that has many dips and bends that need to be navigated with care. So don't think you have to heal yourself in record time; everyone heals in their own time.

10) **Wear your scars with pride.** Don't let those unsightly scars get you down. They are a symbol of your strength and courage, and should be looked upon as a badge of honour.

A near-death experience puts things into perspective. It reminds us that we are not immortal, and that we all have a limited lease on life. It changes the way we think, the way we feel and the outlook we have on life. I certainly became more aware of the things that are important to me such as my health, my family and social awareness, generally.

CHAPTER 31

Simone's battle

Simone Hanley had been in Bali with her sister, Renae Anderson, and a friend – Francoise Dahan – enjoying a long-awaited break. Renae and Francoise had been standing outside the Sari Club when the car bomb went off. They were killed instantly, making them some of the first people to die from the Sari bomb. Simone had been inside the Sari and survived the explosion, albeit with massive burns to her body. Upon arriving in Perth, surgeons tried their best to save her, but her lower left leg continually bled and septicaemia had set in. Her skin grafts were not working and Prof. Wood was preparing to use donor skin grafts, taken from her father but a respiratory infection resulted in the surgery being cancelled. After a courageous 56-day battle, Simone passed away.[43] No-one could even begin to fathom the amount of pain and heartache the Hanley family went through during this stage of their lives, losing both of their daughters in such a cruel manner. When I was told the news of Simone's passing, I was saddened and realised just how lucky I was to have survived.

In the days following Simone's passing, I attended a mass for her in the hospital chapel and after leaving the hospital, I wrote a letter

[43]Rule, B. (2012). 'Bali 10 years on', *The Sunday Times*, 7 October 2012.

to the Hanley family expressing my condolences for the loss of their daughters, and my hope that they could have some comfort knowing that Simone, Renae and Francoise were now together in heaven, looking over them all.

As to what happened to the two Australian girls I was chatting with when the bomb exploded – this remained a mystery to me for some time. Initially I couldn't remember either of their names, but there was one 'clue' that stuck in my mind from the conversation I had with them on the night. I remember the girl sitting next to me telling me that she had moved from the Gold Coast to Sydney, to work as a product development manager for the surf manufacturer Mambo. I later discovered from reading newspaper reports that her name was Julie Stevenson and she had died of her injuries at Bali's Sanglah Hospital, but what happened to her friend is unknown to this day.

What became of Bako? Well Mr Bakovic as I often refer to him, didn't have any physical injuries from the bombings but suffered psychologically from the images he saw on the night. He made several trips to Canada in the years after the bombings to pursue his career in the airline industry. Whilst in Canada he met Melissa Bailot through mutual friend Deanna Thompson, and the two were married in 2013. They have two children named Felix and Anna and live in Calgary, Canada.

CHAPTER 32

Helping with burns research

'The quality of the outcome must be worth the pain of survival'
- Prof. Fiona Wood -[44]

Unfortunately, my family have had a history with fire over the years. On 11 January 1972, four years prior to my birth, two of my little cousins were lost to fire. Victor was aged two years and 10 months, and his sister, Francis, only 16 months old, were incinerated in a car fire. Then in 1979, an arsonist who didn't like foreigners set fire to my family home, burning it to the ground. In 1995, a rental property we owned was badly damaged in a fire caused by a faulty electric blanket. After what happened in Bali in 2002, it seems we've had more than our share of dealings with fire.

When I look back on my survival, I realise that medical science has played an important role. So, when the burn injury research team at RPH asked for volunteers to trial new medical technology for the treatment of burn scarring, I was only too happy to participate.

---

[44]Fiona Wood Foundation website, 'The burns journey',
https://www.fionawoodfoundation.com/what-we-do/the-burns-journey, accessed 11 May 2022.

The research study involved trialling a new machine known as a carbon dioxide laser. At the time, there were only two of these machines in the world: one in Boston, USA, and the other in Perth, Australia. The researchers, consisting of Prof. Fiona Wood, Dr Alexandria Murray and Prof. Suzanne Rea, wanted to assess the effect of the new laser compared to standard scar therapy, to better understand what changes the laser can cause. The study involved three laser treatment operations, each conducted under general anaesthesia over a period of six months, where a patch of scarring on my left arm measuring 5 cm x 5 cm was treated, and the other adjacent scarring left untreated.

Before and after each treatment, high-resolution images were taken of the scarring by PHD students from the University of Western Australia (UWA). They used medical imaging technology known as optical coherence tomography. The imaging technology obtained a detailed image of the skin beneath the surface, which was used to compare the skin before and after the laser treatment. The PHD students developed algorithms, which could count how many blood vessels were in a test patch before and after treatment.

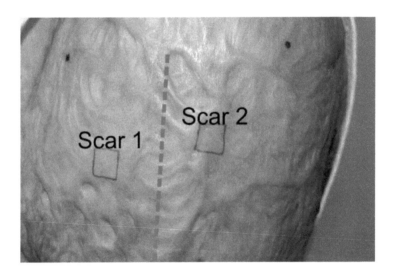

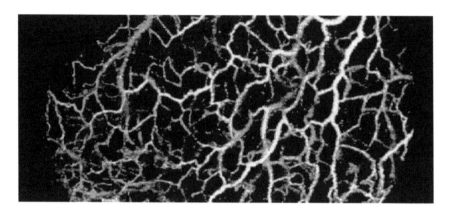

During the study, four scar biopsies taken from me were sent to a lab at UWA for examination by a histopathologist, who analysed the scar for structural changes before and after each laser treatment. The aim of this was to determine what changes the laser caused in the scar tissue.

The carbon dioxide laser beams penetrate the top skin layers, reaching down into the dermis. They create microscopic areas of thermal damage that stimulate new collagen production and replace the damaged skin surface with new epidermal cells.[45]

In terms of risk to me, there was only a small risk of a cold sore developing, which was controlled with a course of antiviral tablets after each treatment. However, the benefits to me included an improvement in the appearance of the scarring and less pain in tight areas. Another, more widespread benefit was that the scientific analysis of the scar biopsy allowed researchers to better understand the effect of carbon dioxide laser treatment, which aided in tailoring laser treatment in the future. This means it is now possible to offer this treatment to a wider group of patients, including children, with troublesome scars. Carbon

[45]Ranaweera, A. (2016). 'Carbon dioxide laser treatment', DermNet NZ, *https://dermnetnz.org/topics/carbon-dioxide-laser-treatment*, accessed 14 February 2022.

dioxide lasers are now a standard part of the treatment for scarring in both adults and children.

For those of us who were in Bali on 12 October 2002, we saw the very worst that humanity has to offer. But in the doctors, nurses, scientists, researchers and other allied health professionals, we also saw the very best that humanity has to offer. These are people who work tirelessly to help the injured to recover. Their job is not easy and they don't receive wide acclaim, but day in and day out they turn up to fight the good fight, to help those who have been dealt a bad hand in life.

Some years later, I did an interview with Channel 7 news presenter Susannah Carr, and as part of the interview I presented Prof. Fiona Wood with an oil painting of a Lotus Flower, which is considered a symbol of rebirth as it rises from darkness and symbolises new life. To this day, it sits proudly on the wall in the burns unit at Fiona Stanley Hospital.

CHAPTER 33

Prof. Fiona Wood

'A truly amazing doctor is hard to find...and impossible to forget.' [46]

Born in 1958 in Hernsworth, Yorkshire England, Prof. Wood commenced her medical career at St Thomas' Hospital Medical School in London, where she found herself drawn to plastic surgery and recognised that she wanted a career that combined research, innovation and surgery. Prof. Wood moved to Australia in 1987, and her dedication to improving outcomes for burns patients and expanding the knowledge of wound healing began in 1991 when she became Western Australia's first female plastic surgeon. Prof. Wood's ability to lead a team and direct innovation for future clinical care was recognised as she quickly became a leader in her field. She became the Director of the Burns Service of Western Australia at an early point in her career. In this position Prof. Wood has led the Burns Service of Western Australia to be recognised internationally as a leader in burns care. [47]

[46]Bhatt, A. (2020). '70 Inspirational Doctor Quotes to Express Your Gratitude', The Random Vibez, 5 August 2020, *https://www.therandomvibez.com/inspirational-doctor-quotes/*, accessed 17 June 2022.
[47]Barry, E. (cont.) (n.d.). 'Professor Fiona Wood, AM, FRCS, FRACS (2 February 1958) PLASTIC & RECONSTRUCTIVE SURGEON', Life on the job. Famous or historic people's stories, *https://www.onthejob.education/life_job/famous_people/Fiona_Wood.htm*, accessed 19 April 2022.

In the days after the Bali bombings, Prof. Wood took charge of the medical response at RPH, with 28 patients to care for. She commanded a team of 19 surgeons and 130 medical staff working around the clock in four theatres, saving many lives. Prof. Wood went on to win a number of awards for her medical achievements, including being named a Member of the Order of Australia (AM) in 2003. In 2003 and 2004, she won the Western Australia Citizen of the Year award for her contribution to medicine in the field of burn research. She was also voted Australia's Most Trusted Person for six successive years (2005–2010) in a *Reader's Digest* poll and has been recognised as an 'Australian Living Treasure'. In 2005, Prof. Wood and Marie Stoner won the Clunies Ross Award (Australian Academy of Technological Sciences and Engineering) for their contributions to medical science in Australia. In 2005 Prof. Wood was named Australian of the Year, and to cap it all off, in 2022 she was awarded the Australian society medal for medical research.

During my last surgery with Prof. Wood on 24 February 2021 she had trainee surgeon Dr Mary in theatre with her. Under Prof. Wood's guidance, Dr Mary carried out three strategic incisions on some troublesome scarring that was causing a restriction of movement in my back. The surgery was a huge success and at my next clinic appointment I joked with both of them that it felt as though I had an empty 'car park' on my back now as I could move more freely. For the plastic surgeons it may just be part and parcel of their job, but for a burn victim to have greater movement is priceless.

To this day, Prof. Wood continues to be a role model to many aspiring doctors, scientists and researchers, and I was very honoured to have had her as my treating doctor.

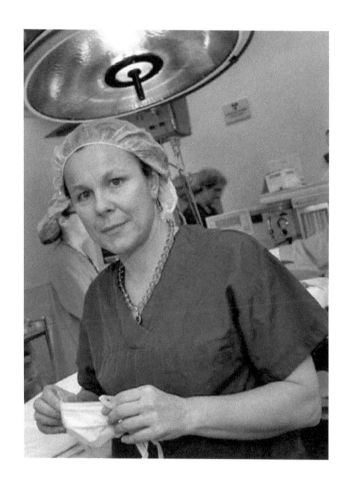

CHAPTER 34

The Bali Peace Park

'True peace is not merely the absence of tension;
it is the presence of justice.'

- Martin Luther King Jr. -

The fate of the land that the Sari Club stood on was the subject of great debate in the aftermath of the tragedy, with many people believing it should be turned into something of significance, to serve as a testimony to those whose lives were cut so tragically short.
In November 2005, the Australian Consulate General in Bali sent a letter to the Regent of Badung (Bupati), requesting information about the use of the former Sari Club site. The Badung Regency Office advised it would be a historical site for displaying documentation, audio videos, photos and books about the bombings. Based on this information, in September 2008 the Bali Peace Park Association Inc (BPPAI) was formed in Perth, with the objective of building a Peace Park on the site of the former Sari Club.

Our cause was supported by then Bali Governor Made Pastika, who advised us that approval to develop the site would only be provided for the Peace Park project.

'We will do all in our power to prevent the building of a nightclub on the site,' he said.

Our Mission Statement was to create a Peace Park on the Sari Club site. Our aim was for people to have a place to reflect upon, and acknowledge, the terrorist attacks on 12 October 2002, along with all acts of terror worldwide. We hoped that this reflection would help build a future without fear, by promoting tolerance, understanding and freedom for generations to come, irrespective of nationality, culture, religious belief or race.

The inaugural president of the association was local Perth journalist Nick Way who took on the task of building a Peace Park in Bali. He was looking for survivors who would be willing to help with the project. I initially met Nick in the aftermath of the 2002 bombings when he worked as a journalist for Channel 10. He covered the 2002 and 2005 bombings. Nick came across as a charismatic type of bloke and had interviewed me for the Chapter 10 documentary *Cry Bali*, which aired on prime-time TV across Australia. Nick invited me to join the association. I agreed to participate in the hope that it would be a good way of turning a negative experience into something positive, whilst at the same time paying tribute to those whose lives were taken.

Even though we had a lot of support for the project in Australia and abroad, the main stumbling block was the reluctance of the landowner to sell the land at a reasonable price. Initially he had asked for $27 million (AUD) for the entire block of 1600m², which was really a 'pie in the sky' amount.

In June 2011, the Australian Government committed $450,000

(AUD) to the project, and the various states and territories committed a further $469,000 (AUD), bringing the total commitment to $919,000 (AUD). This was a far cry from the $27 million (AUD) the landowner wanted, so the challenge for us was to convince a wealthy landowner that his land wasn't worth $27 million (AUD). In 2011, we decided to obtain an independent valuation, just to see what the land was worth so we could use the amount as a bargaining chip. The valuation came in at $900,000 (AUD) based on a non-commercial value.

We presented the valuation to the landowner on the eve of the tenth anniversary in 2012, but he wouldn't have a bar of it; he was adamant the land was worth more but dropped his asking price to $7.2 million (AUD). To complicate matters further, he wanted to take a 100m² slice of the land for access to a restaurant at the rear of the property.

In October 2013, the then Australian PM Tony Abbott visited the Sari site, and he and Governor Made Pastika reaffirmed their support for the Peace Park.

For the Balinese, the bomb site was an eyesore, with many of the locals supporting a park being built on the site and, indeed, the local Banjars (Mayors) of the various districts were very supportive of the Peace Park. Faced with mounting pressure the landowner was starting to become nervous and in September 2014, he contacted the Banjar of the Kuta district and told him he was willing to negotiate a partial sale of the land: 600m² of the total 1600m² at the front of the block, across from the main monument.

On 21 January 2015, a delegation from the committee held meetings with Governor Made Pastika in Denpasar. The meeting was very positive, with Governor Pastika reaffirming his support for the project and appointing one of his senior officers to help with the negotiations. In fact, Governor Pastika made it clear to everyone at the meeting of his displeasure at seeing the Sari site in such a dilapidated state. A few days later, the delegation met with the landowner's representative, Pak Dewa Jatinegara, in Denpasar with the aim of thrashing out a deal. The talks were very positive and covered the option of leasing the land as well as an outright purchase. Pak Dewa said he would discuss this with the landowner and get back to the association within a fortnight to outline the landowner's offer.

On 16 February 2015, the BPPAI received a letter from the landowner, which stated that the land was worth \$80,000 (AUD) per square metre, which meant the 600m^2 of land was worth \$4.8 million (AUD). The landowner said this was the average price of other properties in the Kuta area; however, he did not say whether these prices were for commercial or non-commercial land. The association considered his offer and, realising it was still too high, made a counteroffer of \$900,000 (AUD) on 1 April 2015. The offer was based on a non-commercial valuation of the land and although it was considerably less than what the landowner was asking, it was all we had to offer. The landowner flatly refused our offer and stated that he didn't want to hear back from us ever again. This was a major setback in our efforts to purchase the land and made us think long and hard about the project and whether we should continue with it. Although we were all motivated, there was no way we could raise \$4.8 million (AUD) to meet the landowner's demands, so we had to devise a new strategy to try to obtain the land.

In December 2015, committee members Nick Way and Alistair Lyon travelled to Bali to meet with a Balinese senator named Wedakarna, after receiving an invitation from him. Senator Wedakarna had attended the thirteenth anniversary service in Kuta and was informed of the Peace Park project by our local community liaison officer, Ayu Winastri. The meeting with Senator Wedakarna was very positive and he agreed to raise the issue with President Joko

Widodo in Jakarta, as well as speak directly to the landowner to see if he would sell at a lower price. Unfortunately, Senator Wedakarna did not fulfil his promise and, like a lot of politicians, he appeared to be full of hot air. In fact, the only time the Balinese politicians spoke with us was when we instigated the discussions, which was disappointing.

To help influence the landowner from an emotional perspective, we enlisted the support of the Isana Dewata Foundation, which represented 53 Balinese families directly affected by the bombings. Gaining support from the locals was crucial, as it showed that it wasn't just Australians who wanted a Peace Park but the Balinese as well.

On 12 October 2017, the association received notification from the Australian Consul General in Bali that an IMB (building permit) had been issued for the Sari site, but that the governor had spoken to the Regent (Bupati) and asked him not to approve any development.

A new direction

The IMB had ruffled our feathers and it was becoming clear that we needed a new strategy to combat the underhanded dealings of the landowner. Although Nick Way had done a great job of keeping the Peace Park alive, he was now based in Canberra working as a media consultant for the Minister for Ageing and therefore no longer able to devote enough time to the project. It was decided that David Napoli would take on the chairperson role. David, an astute businessman, knew that we needed to act quickly before the landowner could use his influence to coerce the Bupati into providing another IMB. Hence, David enlisted the support of new Australian Consul General Dr Helena Studdert, who was based in Bali. Dr Studdert, a former member of the Australian Army and a Kalgoorlie girl at heart, was keen to assist and said that she wanted to build the Peace Park before her tenure ended. This was just the ticket we needed: someone who

could ruffle some diplomatic feathers and get things moving. Dr Studdert wasted no time and was soon organising meetings with the new Governor Koster, the Bupati, the Isana Dewata Foundation, and various other politicians.

In October 2018, she organised a Counter-Terrorism Summit in Bali, which was to provide the impetus for further discussion on the Peace Park. I attended the event with my brother, Glen, and we both gave speeches at the summit.

Dr Studdert later stated, 'The presentation given by Antony and his brother, Glen, was very effective in driving home the importance Australia attaches to the incident site.'

By November 2018, we were starting to get a clearer picture of the state of play in Bali. Dr Studdert met with the landowner's new representative, a lady by the name of Ibu Tania, who claimed to be the landowner's niece, and Pak Badra, who was head of Bali

Tourism. Ibu Tania had only come onto the scene recently, and she made the startling claim that none of the previous negotiations had been authorised by the landowner, but most importantly she shared the land certificate for the Sari site. This was the first time we had seen the land title and it gave us confidence that we were now dealing with the right person.

Hence, now that we had a clear and direct line to the landowner, the BPPAI realised it was the time to act and offered $2 million (AUD) for the Sari site. Ibu Tania advised she would speak with the landowner and get back to us by the end of December 2018 with an answer. As the date got closer, Ibu Tania kept holding off on meeting by making all sorts of excuses. By the end of January 2019, it was becoming clear that something wasn't quite right, and the landowner was using stalling tactics.

In March 2019, things suddenly took a turn for the worst. Ibu Tania contacted us through the Australian Consulate and informed us that an IMB had once again been issued for the site, to Hotel Cianjur Asri for a five-storey development encompassing a monument and restaurant, and that we could have access to the fifth floor of the development for a 100-year lease of $4.8 million (AUD) per annum to establish a rooftop Peace Park. We were absolutely gobsmacked and an urgent meeting of the committee was called to decide what to do next. It appeared the landowner had done a secret deal with the Bupati, and with construction set to commence on 4 April 2019, we had to act fast to stop the development.

In the week of 31 March 2019, BPPAI Chairperson David Napoli boarded a flight to Bali on a mercy mission to have the development stopped. David worked quickly to set up a meeting with new Bali Governor Koster, who offered to seek a stay on the development and agreed to call the landowner to his office as soon as possible.

David also met with Ibu Tania, Dr Helena Studdert, Pak Badra and Isana Dewata representative Lina Marupinga on the morning of Thursday 4 April, to discuss the IMB. It was clear that the IMB was required to make provision for the Peace Park, and in Ibu Tania's mind she had done so. It was also obvious that the Badung Regency had signed off on the IMB because the rear half of the site would be a multi-storey car park, which would likely profit the Badung Regency. The front block would be a food hall and restaurant. During the meeting, questions started to emerge about who actually owned the land and why the IMB was issued to the Hotel Cianjur Asri. David informed Ibu Tania that a lease of the fifth floor of the development was not an option from a victims' point of view and that a $4.8 million (AUD) lease was not viable. He also advised her that the BPPAI was left with little option but to seek a political intervention.

This was more than just a planning issue; it was about Bali's reputation as a tourist destination. If we'd had to walk away, it would have created bad publicity in Australia – a source of 1.5 million visitors each year. There were many other countries watching the progress of achieving a Peace Park on the site of the Sari Club.

That afternoon, David met with Brigadier General Herwan Chaidir (dec.), Head of Indonesia's Anti-Terrorism Unit, and his two advisers. I had previously met the general at the Counter-Terrorism Summit in October 2018, and saw that he was very well respected amongst the Balinese community. They were extremely helpful and encouraging. One of the advisers had been raised in the US and spoke perfect English, and had a legal background. The general offered to investigate the ownership of the land and meet with the Bupati. It was also suggested that the community start a class action to prevent the construction, by seeking a withdrawal of the permit. Class actions to the Administrative Court do not incur costs. The general and his colleagues would seek to influence the local community to oppose the permit and support the park. The general said he would find out who issued the IMB.

Ibu Tania had learned of David's meeting with General Herwan Chaidir and asked for a meeting with him, herself, on that Thursday evening. Unbeknown to her, Lina and David were also invited. After about three hours of negotiation, she indicated a willingness to sell the front 600 metres, subject to agreement from the family. David made it clear that it had to be a realistic figure and not some 'pie in the sky' amount.

Back in Australia, BPPAI Secretary, Keith Pearce, organised an English Tea at the Kingsley Memorial Rooms on 14 April 2019, to raise some funds for the project. He invited numerous politicians from a state and federal level to the event. Dr Anne Ally, who was the shadow member for Cowan and a counter-terrorism expert, gave an outstanding speech on the merits of the Peace Park. Gaining the support of politicians was crucial in obtaining more funding for our project, and it set the foundation for us to approach federal finance minister Mathias Cormann to provide some more funding. David had good links with Mathias, but we had to act fast as the government had called an election for 18 May 2019, and further funding commitments cannot be approved in the four weeks leading up to an election.

More funding was crucial to obtain the land, but it wasn't going to stop Ibu Tania. In the three weeks since we'd last spoken to her, there was movement on the ground in Bali. The IMB had once again been enacted by God knows who, and it was on again. The stall holders who had occupied the former Sari site were told to pack up their belongings and vacate the site by 28 April 2019, as work was set to commence on 1 May 2019. Word soon filtered through to Australia and all hell broke loose. The media caught hold of the story and soon there was public outrage from all survivors about the impending five-storey development. News stories ran on talkback radio shows and appeared in newspapers and on TV.

Prime Minister Scott Morrison piped up and said he was deeply concerned by the fact that a five-storey building was going to be built on the site. Whilst he was in Perth, on Tuesday 30 April 2019, in the middle of his election campaign, the PM met with survivors at a private function and told them they had his full support; he also instructed Chairperson David Napoli to go back to Bali and negotiate a settlement.

With public pressure mounting, the Indonesian Consul General in Perth, Dewi Gustina Tobing, phoned Chairperson David Napoli and told him the development had been stopped and she would help him broker a deal with the landowner in Bali. The stage was set and 6 May 2019 was going to be D-Day.

By this stage we had stopped the development twice in the space of two months and pressure was mounting on Ibu Tania. On 2 May 2019, a meeting was called with Governor Koster in Bali. Also present at the meeting were Australian Consul General, Dr Helena Studdert; Ibu Lina (Isana Dewata Foundation); Ibu Wayan (one of the victims); and representatives from Badung Regency.

Three key points were raised at the meeting:

1. Based on the information from Governor Koster, the landowner agreed to postpone the construction, to give time for a discussion between the landowner and the BPPAI to get a fair deal.

2. The governor advised us he had met with Dewa Jatinegara (the landowner's new representative), who told him that he had met and discussed the issue with the BPPAI.

3. Dewa Jatinegara also informed Governor Koster that the landowner had agreed that the BPPAI could buy the land and build the memorial. But after a 'long time' there was no update and no confirmation from the BPPAI and therefore the owner had decided to apply for an IMB and build on his land.

Obviously point three was a lie, because even though we had met with the landowner's representative, we had never heard back from him on our last offer in November 2018. We also knew the landowner had used stalling tactics to distract us whilst he obtained an IMB on the land.

During the meeting Governor Koster provided three options:

1. That the BPPAI buy the 600m² block of land based on market price.

2. That government-owned land in the area of 820m², which is located on Jalan Sriwijaya, 1.5km away from the location of Bali bombings, be exchanged with the landowner's site, if the landowner did not want to sell. If costs were incurred, these would be paid by the BPPAI.

3. If those two options failed, then the government would donate their land to the BPPAI to build the memorial.

The issue with not meeting directly with the landowner at any stage was an interesting one. Word on the street was that he had never paid taxes on the Sari site and therefore wouldn't step foot in Bali for fear of being arrested, but this theory was later dispelled because the Bupati would never have approved an IMB if he owed back taxes. Rumours of Mafia involvement in the ill-fated Sari Club were also present, but why the landowner never met with us or any other government official remains a mystery.

David arrived in Bali on 6 May 2019 and had a meeting the next day with Ibu Tania and various other government officials. By the end of the meeting the landowner had agreed to sell the land for $4.8 million (AUD), but there was a catch. The landowner now wanted us to pay $9 million (AUD) in compensation for lost earnings for the 17 years the former Sari site lay idle. Just when we thought a deal was done, they threw a curve ball into the mix just to try to unsettle us again. Not only was it impossible for us to pay compensation, but it would make it look as though we were responsible for the bombings rather than the terrorists, so this was most certainly a no-deal for us.

Although we had been dealing with Ibu Tania for some time, we eventually found out she wasn't the niece of the owner at all, but rather a selling agent who wanted to earn a healthy commission from the sale of the Sari site. When we discovered this, we severed ties with her and discovered the real owner of the site was Mr Sukamto Jamhur.

On 19 November 2019, the BPPAI made a counteroffer direct to Sukamto to buy the land for $4.5 million (AUD) for 1500m^2, with no compensation for lost earnings. The landowner refused the offer and came back asking for $4.4 million (AUD) for a lease of 480m^2 for a period of 99 years, or $6.5 million (AUD) for a lease of 560m^2, or, if we wanted to purchase the land outright, he wanted $10.2 million (AUD) with a down payment straight away. There was no way in the world we could pay this amount of money.

The negotiations for the Peace Park must have been one of the most drawn-out and complicated negotiations since the signing of the Treaty of Versailles. To this day there is still no deal reached and in November 2021, the association made the difficult decision to withdraw from the negotiations all together.

It was clear that the landowners were dragging out the negotiations for as long as possible to put us off the trail, so they could build their new five-storey entertainment complex. Back in Australia, opinion was split over whether a park should be built or if the family should be able to do what they want with their land. Initially I was disappointed about the failure of the Peace Park, especially given the amount of time and effort that so many people had put into the project.

Over the years, the relationship between Australia and Indonesia has had its ups and downs, from the issues associated with terrorism, the Balibo 5, Australia's involvement in liberating East Timor and publicity associated with drug runners. The Bali Peace Park would have been a great example of cooperation towards peace, but it wasn't to be.

I have come to accept that only loss has resulted from the terror attacks in Bali: many people lost loved ones in the attack, the Balinese economy was destroyed overnight, costing thousands of people their livelihoods; survivors are still healing from their wounds; the owners of the two bars lost a lot of money; the three main perpetrators were executed; and the people who planned the attack spent time in jail. The failure to bring the Peace Park to fruition is just the latest one.

CONCLUSION

'After the rain, the sun will re-appear. There is life.
After the pain, the joy will still be here'.

- Walt Disney -[48]

There is no doubt that a burn injury has the potential to be a soul-destroying injury. However, with careful management and support, you can recover and go on to lead a relatively normal, happy and fulfilled life.

I hope this book has provided some inspiration to those of you who have suffered the indignity of a burn injury but had the good fortune to survive it.

---

[48]Disney, W. (n.d.). Quote Fancy, *https://quotefancy.com/quote/930218/Walt-Disney-After-the-rain-the-sun-will-reappear-There-is-life-After-the-pain-the-joy*, accessed 28 June 2022.

ACKNOWLEDGEMENTS

Throughout our lives, we all need someone to guide and support us. Those people are often our parents. For me, this is true, my parents brought me into this world through an act of love, and they will love me unconditionally for the rest of their lives. Hence, it would be remiss of me not to mention the role my parents have played in my life. Both my parents migrated to Australia in the early 1960s and set about raising a family with very little knowledge of the English language or the Australian lifestyle. They had to work hard over the years to establish themselves in this country, which didn't always treat them well. In those days foreigners where racially abused in the streets and my parents had their first home destroyed by an arsonist who hated foreigners. Despite this setback they continued to work hard, often having to work two jobs to make ends meet – life was a struggle.

In the 1980s, when interest rates were around the 18 per cent mark, most of their money went into paying off the mortgage. Despite how hard my parents had to work, they just got on with it without a fuss. I have many fond memories of coming home from school, only to hop into the family station wagon and head off for an evening of cleaning offices in Fremantle. My job was to empty all the rubbish bins, which I would knock over fairly quickly.

This early introduction to work instilled discipline in my character, and I learned from an early age that you have to work hard to achieve something in life. I feel grateful for the hard work our parents did to provide for us, and to nurture us during our lives. All I can do is say a heartfelt Thank You.

Despite my brush with death, I truly believe there are more good people in this world than there are bad, and I have been lucky enough to come into contact with some of the best over the years. Amongst them, the tireless workers of the Fiona Wood Foundation, who have certainly improved outcomes for burn survivors throughout the world.

To help with the ongoing research into burn treatment, I am donating 50% of proceeds from the sale of this book to the Fiona Wood Foundation, as it is only through research that we can unlock the mystery of a burn injury and continue to make improvements to the treatment available.

A special thank you to Tracey Everson (*Fine Detail Editing*) for editing of the original manuscript, Sally Asnicar (*Full Proof Reading Services*) for the proof read, and Michelle Holyhead (*The Book Studio*) for the formatting and production of this book.

On this note, I would like to say thank you for taking the time to read my story. I hope you have enjoyed the book and that you experience safe travels in your journey of life.

Terima Khasi.
Antony Svilicich

If you would like to remain in contact, follow me on:
- https://www.facebook.com/bali2002survivor
- https://www.linkedin.com/feed/
- https://www.instagram.com/asvilicich/
- https://www.youtube.com/channel/UCmeHKK-R5eKeekx_m514Yxw

LIST OF REFERENCES

Ashok, I. (2017). '"Where there is life there is hope" – Stephen Hawking shares incredibly inspiring life lessons', International Business Times, 23 November 2017, *https://www.ibtimes.co.uk/where-there-life-there-hope-stephen-hawking-shares-incredibly-inspiring-life-lessons-1648595*, accessed 29 June 2022.

Barry, E. (cont.) (n.d.). 'Professor Fiona Wood, AM, FRCS, FRACS (2 February 1958–) PLASTIC & RECONSTRUCTIVE SURGEON', Life on the job. Famous or historic people's stories, *https://www.onthejob.education/life_job/famous_people/Fiona_Wood.htm*, accessed 19 April 2022.

Bhatt, A., (2020). '70 Inspirational Doctor Quotes to Express Your Gratitude',

The Random Vibez, 5 August 2020, *https://www.therandomvibez.com/inspirational-doctor-quotes/*, accessed 17 June 2022.

Boskey, E. (2020). Uses for Integra Skin Graft Substitute: Integra helps regrow skin after burns or reconstructive surgery, Verywell Health, 19 March 2020, *https://www.verywellhealth.com/integra-skin-graft-4796663*, accessed 23 May 2022.

Burn Injury Guide, 'Burn Sepsis' (n.d.), *https://burninjuryguide.com/burn-recovery/burn-complications/burn-sepsis/*, accessed 30 June 2022.

Centre for Disease Control and Prevention (n.d.). 'Pseudomonas aeruginosa in Healthcare Settings', *https://www.cdc.gov/hai/organisms/pseudomonas.html*, accessed 23 May 2021.

Clinical Trials.gov, (n.d.). 'Treatment for Malignant Ovarian Cancer: Laparoscopy vs Laparotomy', U.S. National Library of Medicine, *https://clinicaltrials.gov/ct2/show/NCT02686463*, accessed 31 May 2022.

Course Hero (n.d.). 'Anatomy and Physiology I, Module 6: The Integumentary System Diseases, Disorders, and Injuries', *https://www.coursehero.com/study-guides/austincc-ap1/diseases-disorders-and-injuries-of-the-integumentary-system/*, accessed 11 May 2022.

Disney, W. (n.d.). Quote Fancy, *https://quotefancy.com/quote/930218/Walt-Disney-After-the-rain-the-sun-will-reappear-There-is-life-After-the-pain-the-joy,* accessed 28 June 2022.

Edgar, S., (2021). 'The benefits of volunteering for your mental health', 6 July 2021, Lifeline WA, *https://wa.lifeline.org.au/resources/helpful-articles/the-benefits-of-volunteering-for-your-mental-health/,* accessed 26 June 2022.

Fiona Wood Foundation. 'Our challenge', *https://www.fionawoodfoundation.com/what-we-do/our-challenge,* accessed 11 May 2022.

Fiona Wood Foundation. 'The burns journey', *https://www.fionawoodfoundation.com/what-we-do/the-burns-journey,* accessed 11 May 2022.

Forbes M, Silvester J. (2003). 'How they got the bombers', The Age, 6 October 2003, *https://www.theage.com.au/national/how-they-got-the-bombers-20031006-gdwhid.html,* accessed 11 October 2003.

Goodsir, D. (2003). 'The night terror touched our lives', The Age, 4 October 2003, *https://www.theage.com.au/national/the-night-terror-touched-our-lives-20031004-gdwgk8.html,* accessed 11 October 2003.

Guy-Evans, O. (2021). 'Amygdala function and location', Simply Psychology, 9 May 2021, *www.simplypsychology.org/amygdala.html,* accessed 27 June 2022.

Guy-Evans, O. (2021). 'Amygdala Hijack and the Fight or Flight Response', Simply Psychology, 5 November 2021, *www.simplypsychology.org/what-happens-during-an-amygdala-hijack.html,* accessed 27 June 2022.

Harris, R. (2011) 'Embracing Your Demons: An Overview of Acceptance and Commitment Therapy', 2011, Psychotherapy.net, *https://www.psychotherapy.net/article/Acceptance-and-Commitment-Therapy-ACT,* accessed 27 June 2021.

Harris, Dr R. (2009). 'Mindfulness without meditation', HCPJ, October 2009, *https://www.actmindfully.com.au/upimages/Mindfulness_without_meditation_--_Russ_Harris_--_HCPJ_Oct_09.pdf,* accessed 20 May 2022.

Healthline (2017). 'EFT Tapping', *https://www.healthline.com/health/eft-tapping,* accessed 11 December 2021.

Heath, Dr J. (n.d.). 'Trauma', *https://www.janheath.com.au/clinical-services/trauma/*, accessed 16 September 2021.

Howard, J. (2012). 'Weekend Insight - Bali 10 years on', Sunday Times, 7 October 2012.

Johnson, S. (1998). Who Moved My Cheese? An Amazing Way to Deal with Change in Your Work and in Your Life, Putnam Adult (New York City, New York, USA)

MedlinePlus (n.d.). 'Shock', National Library of Medicine, *https://medlineplus.gov/shock.html*, accessed 11 May 2022.

National Social Anxiety Center (n.d.). 'Public Speaking Anxiety', *https://nationalsocialanxietycenter.com/social-anxiety/public-speaking-anxiety/*, accessed 30 June 2022.

Noble, T. (2003). 'How dozens of lives were saved in the flight of Bali', The Age, 5 October 2003, *https://www.theage.com.au/national/how-dozens-of-lives-were-saved-in-the-flight-of-bali-20031005-gdwhbs.html*, accessed 11 October 2003.

Pittman, S. (2020). 'New study suggests people have more than 6000 thoughts per day', 16 July 2020, The Mighty, *https://themighty.com/2020/07/study-how-many-thoughts-per-day/*, accessed 26 June 2020.

Pueblo, Y. (n.d.), located at D. Sy on Pinterest, *https://www.pinterest.com.au/pin/358317714104584506/*, accessed 5 May 2022.

Ranaweera, A. (2016). 'Carbon dioxide laser treatment', DermNet NZ, *https://dermnetnz.org/topics/carbon-dioxide-laser-treatment*, accessed 14 February 2022.

Reavley, N., Morgan, A., Jorm, A., Wright, J., Bassilios, B., Hopwood, M., Allen, N. & **Purcell, R.** (2010). A Guide to What Works for Anxiety Disorders, beyondblue: Melbourne 2010, *https://learn.beyondblue-elearning.org.au/workplace/resources/pdf/topic5/GuideToWhatWorksForAnxiety.pdf*, accessed 5 February 2021.

Robinson, L., Segal, J. & **Smith, M.** (2021). 'Help Guide - The Mental Health Benefits of Exercise', HelpGuide, August 2021, *https://www.helpguide.org/articles/healthy-living/the-mental-health-benefits-of-exercise.htm?platform=hootsuite&pdf=13390*, accessed 25 June 2022.

Rule, B. (2012). 'Bali 10 years on', The Sunday Times, 7 October 2012.

Taylor, G. (2003). 'Resolving Trauma with EMDR', Pathways of Mind website, *https://pathwaysofmind.com/healing-from-trauma/emdr/graham-taylor-resolving-trauma-with-emdr/*, accessed 4 October 2021.

Tolle, E. (2005). A New Earth: Awakening to Your Life's Purpose, Viking Press (New York City, New York, USA).

'Triumphant Bali survivor limps home for a coldie', The Age, 7 January 2003, *https://www.theage.com.au/national/triumphant-bali-survivor-limps-home-for-a-coldie-20030107-gdv166.html*, accessed 27 June, 2018.

Williams, C. (2008). 'Parkland formula – fluid resuscitation in burns patients 1: Using formulas', Nursing Times, 104:14, 28–29.

Wong, K. (2002). ICU Discharge Summary, Royal Perth Hospital, 25 November 2002.

World Health Organization (2022). 'Mental health: strengthening our response', *https://www.who.int/news-room/fact-sheets/detail/mental-health-strengthening-our-response*, accessed 5 January 2021.

IN MEMORIAM

In memory of the 202 victims of the 2002 Bali bombings

AUSTRALIA: 88

Gayle Airlie
Belinda Allen
Renae Anderson
Peter Basioli
Christina Betmilik
Matthew Bolwerk
Abbey Borgia
Debbie Borgia
Gerardine Buchan
Steve Buchan
Chloe Byron
Anthony Cachia
Rebecca Cartledge
Bronwyn Cartwright
Jodie Cearns
Jane Corteen
Jenny Corteen
Paul Cronin
Donna Croxford
Kristen Curnow
Francoise Dahan
Sylvia Dalais
Joshua Deegan

Andrew Dobson
Michelle Dunlop
Craig Dunn
Shane Foley
Dean Gallagher
Angela Golotta
Angela Gray
Byron Hancock
Simone Hanley
James Hardman
Billy Hardy
Nicole Harrison
Tim Hawkins
Andrea Hore
Adam Howard
Paul Hussey
Josh Iliffe
Carol Johnstone
David Kent
Dimmy Kotronakis
Elizabeth Kotronakis
Aaron Lee
Justin Lee
Stacey Lee

Danny Lewis
Scott Lysaght
Linda Makawana
Sue Maloney
Robert Marshall
David Mavroudis
Lynette McKeon
Marissa McKeon
Jenny Murphy
Amber O'Donnell
Jessica O'Donnell
Sue Ogier
Jodie O'Shea
Corey Paltridge
Charles van Renen
Brad Ridley
Ben Roberts
Bronwyn Ross
David Ross
Kathy Salvatori
Greg Sanderson
Cathy Seelin
Lee Sexton
Tom Singer
Anthony Stewart
Julie Stevenson
Jason Stokes
Behic Sumer

Nathan Swaine
Tracy Thomas
Clint Thompson
Robert Thwaites
Jonathan Wade
Vanessa Walder
Jodie Wallace
Shane Walsh-Till
Robyn Webster
Marlene Whiteley
Charmaine Whitton
Gerard Yeo
Luiza Zervos

INDONESIA: 38

I Wayan Yustara
R Destria Bimo Adhi Wibowo
Ni Kadek Alit Margarini
Gusti Ayu Made Artini
Arsoyo Rahmat
I Made Wija
I Ketut Nana Wijaya
I Nyoman Mawa
Elly Susanti Suharto
I Wayan Sukadana
I Ketut Cindra
Ati Savitri
I Ketut Sumarawat

I Gede Badrawan
Hanny
I Made Wijaya
I Komang Candra
Tata Duka
Lilis Puspita
Jonathan Simanjuntak
I Made Mertana
I Made Sujana
Salwindar Singh
Juniardi
I Kadek Ngartina
I Wayan Tamba
Rudy Armansyah
Mochamad Khotib
Imawan Sardjono
Endang
Mugianto
Widayati
Faturrahman
Achmad Suharto
Arismanandar
Agus Suheri
Kadek Sukerna
I Kadek Beni Prima

UNITED KINGDOM: 23
Timothy John Arnold
Neil Bowler
Daniel Braden
Christopher Bradford
Jonathon Ellwood
Lucy S.O. Empson
Ian Findley
Emma Louise Fox
Laura France
Marc Gajardo
Tom Holmes
Paul Martin Hussey
Christopher John Kays
Annika Kerstin Linden
Dan (Nathaniel) Miller
Natalie Perkins
Peter Record
Christian Redman
Stevie Speirs
Michael Standring
Ed Waller
Clive John Walton
Douglas Warner

UNITED STATES: 7

Megan Eileen Heffernan
Deborah Lea Snodgrass
Karri Jane Casner
George Hamilton Milligan
Robert Alan McCormick II
Steven Brooks Webster
Jacob Cardwell Young

SWEDEN: 5

Linda Cronqvist
Ulrika Gustafsson
Maria Johansson
Johanna Bergander
Carina Rafling

GERMANY: 6

Marie Cecile Wendt
Angelika Helene Kohnke
Caludia Dietlinde Thiele
Bettina Christina Brandes
Alexandra Koppke
Udo Paul Hauke

NETHERLANDS: 4

Norbet Edgar Freriks
Sander Harskamp
Mark Antonio Schippers
Marjanne Van Lijen Noomen

FRANCE: 4

Guillaume Breant
Lionel Erisey
Manuel Mordelet
Anthony Underwood

NEW ZEALAND: 2

Mark Parker
Jamie Wellington

DENMARK: 3

Lise Tanghus Knudsen
Laerke Cecile Bodker
Anette Overgaard Jensen

SWITZERLAND: 3

Serina Leish
Michale Pascal Dolf
Andrea Gian Rupp

JAPAN: 2

Kosuke Suzuki
Yuka Suzuki

SOUTH AFRICA: 2

Godfrey Fitz
Craig Russel Harty

SOUTH KOREA: 2
Moon Eun-Young
Moon Eun-Jung

CANADA: 2
Richard Gleason
Mervin Popadynec

BRAZIL: 2
Alexandre Moraes Watake
Sargento Marco Antonio Farias

GREECE: 1
Dimitris N Panagoulas

POLAND: 1
Daneta Beata Pawlak

PORTUGAL: 1
Diogo Miguel dantas
Riberinho

ITALY: 1
Antonio Roberto Sbironi

ECUADOR: 1
Ana Cecilia Aviles

TAIWAN: 1
Miss Hui-Min Kuo

UNKNOWN: 2

CPSIA information can be obtained
at www.ICGtesting.com
Printed in the USA
BVHW020958051022
648621BV00032B/1315